GRAND DUCHY
OF WARSAW
AUSTRIAN
EMPIRE
Black Sea
TURKISH
EMPIRE
Corfu
Crete
Cyprus
Mediterranean Sea
EGYPT

MAIDA: A FORGOTTEN VICTORY

Major General Sir John Stuart. Stipple engraving by Anthony Cardon after William Wood (courtesy of the Director, National Army Museum)

Maida: A Forgotten Victory

by

JOHN STEWART

The Pentland Press
Edinburgh – Cambridge – Durham – USA

First published in 1997 by
The Pentland Press Ltd
1 Hutton Close
South Church
Bishop Auckland
Durham

ISBN 1–85821-476-9

Typeset by Carnegie Publishing, 18 Maynard St, Preston
Printed and bound by Antony Rowe Ltd, Chippenham

Contents

Illustrations and Maps

Illustrations

Maps

Foreword

When, thirty-seven years ago, I first came to live within two hundred yards of Maida Vale, the name meant nothing to me; a few days later, however, I found myself walking past a pub called *The Hero of Maida*, bearing on its sign a portrait clearly labelled 'Sir John Stuart'. Then, and only then, did I take down *A Dictionary of Battles* by David Eggenberger – a work which, if you share my passion for reference books, I cannot recommend too highly – from which I learnt that Maida was in fact a small battle fought on a sweltering morning in July 1806 between the British and French in Calabria, a region which I had never previously suspected of having been a Napoleonic theatre of war.

A small battle, but a considerable victory – which was, incidentally, the first we could claim to have won on European soil since the French Revolution: a victory in which a British army, fighting with exemplary courage, defeated a French force a quarter as large again; in which the French casualties amounted to well over two thousand, the British to just 327. On the lighter side, it also marked the occasion when, for the first time since antiquity, a fully-armed brigade fell into line of battle stark naked and when, probably for the first time in all history, the alleged indecency of the Scottish kilt was the subject of a formal protest by an archbishop.

None of this should I ever have known without the book you now hold in your hands. Thanks to its author, the forgotten victory of his sub-title need be forgotten no longer. And I for one shall feel a tiny, vicarious thrill of pride every time I walk past *The Hero of Maida* to catch the bus.

John Julius Norwich

Acknowledgements

My first acknowledgement must be to James Irvine-Robertson, a descendent of the sister of General David Stewart of Garth and Drumcharry, for having allowed me to reproduce family papers giving the General's hitherto unpublished account of his part in the battle. He was at the time a major and second-in-command of the 2/78th Highlanders. Being unwilling to risk damaging the reputation of people still alive had caused him to keep his accounts secret.

The support of Dr Peter Boyden and his staff in the National Army Museum has been invaluable and I must also express appreciation of the helpfulness of the staff at the Perth Public Library – formerly the Sandeman, now the A.K. Bell Library. They have been patient with my enquiries for books long out of print and assiduous in locating copies.

Mr Hans Norton of the Paddington Waterways and Maida Vale Society has been of much help in lending me photographs of Maida Vale showing the former pub (first licensed in 1810) called 'The Hero of Maida'. How sad that it should no longer exist as a pub. Miss Lindsey Macfarlane of the National Maritime Museum most kindly sent me a long list of prints and drawings held in Greenwich and helped me choose three which are reproduced as illustrations.

Three personal friends read my text and made suggestions which I acted on. I wish to acknowledge my gratitude to them: Robert Horan; Lieutenant Colonel William Macnair, late Queen's Own Highlanders; Dr R.S. Smart, until recently Keeper of manuscripts and University muniments at St Andrews.

Finally I wish to express thanks for the generous support received by my sister Elizabeth, who sadly died before she could see the book in print.

J.W.S.
February 1997

Introduction

The battle of Maida was the first victory since the French Revolution of the British army on the mainland of Europe where it had experienced a series of reverses. Sir Walter Scott called it

a new dawn:
And Maida's myrtles gleamed beneath its ray
Where first the soldiers stung with generous shame,
Rivalled the heroes of the watery way,
And washed in foeman's gore unjust reproach away.

The large staghound sitting beside Sir Walter in Landseer's famous portrait was called Maida, and was a gift to Scott from Macdonell of Glengarry who had fought at Maida. The dog became so bored with being painted that Scott said he used to leave the room when he saw an artist putting up his easel.

Despite its great impact on the public at home in 1806, the battle soon became eclipsed in memory by larger-scale victories. William Windham, Secretary of State for War, put it in historical perspective:

> The military renown of our later days dates from our achievements in Egypt: that the battle of Maida confirmed it; and that the battles of Vimeiro, Corunna and Talavera were worth a whole archipelago of those sugar islands in the West Indies in the reduction of which we had been dribbling away our troops.

Today, how many Londoners know the reason for the name Maida Vale? Perhaps through my life-long admiration for Sir Walter Scott I have always been interested in the battle. No easily available book has been written about it, so I have attempted to fill the gap by putting together accounts by people who were actually there. These are mostly to be found in published memoirs and letters but I have also had access to some family papers left by David Stewart of Garth which include a memorandum written by him the year before his death telling a story which he had kept secret during the lifetime of officers whose reputation might be harmed by its being known. Thanks to the National Army Museum, I have also seen an unpublished letter written by Sir John Stuart the day after the battle to his second-in-command left in Sicily.

I have paid a short visit to Calabria to look at the battle-field. The village of St Eufemia near where the British landed has now become a large town, La Mezia. It has three parts, in shape slightly resembling a shamrock. La Mezia Terme has a mainline station on the way between Rome and Reggio di Calabria. There is the beginning of tourist development along its beaches. The other parts of La Mezia spread inland onto the fertile central plain. The two towns, Nicastro on the north, Maida on the south, each about 1000 ft. above sea-level, are clearly visible. The Lamato river which flows down the valley from near Maida cannot have changed much over the centuries, but in places it has been trained so its sides are less boggy. The ruined tower near which the army landed still stands, the Bastione di Malta. It is now about a mile from the beach, so the Tyrrhenian must have receded since 1806 when the British made it the centre of a defence work, surrounded with a ditch and a semi-circle of sandbags touching the shore at both ends. In the town of Maida I chanced to meet a local man who knew of the battle and directed me to a house where a picture of it is hanging. He knew that it had given its name to a district of London.

J. W. S.
Comrie
1993

Chapter One

Setting the scene

The long war with France which followed the French Revolution began when the French annexed Belgium and Holland and presented a threat to British trade. Pitt had been Prime Minister since 1783 and he was to be the most persistent of the allied leaders opposing French expansion. Napoleon, who first came to fame at the siege of Toulon in 1793, quickly recognized England as his most dangerous enemy. England, 'a nation of shopkeepers', depended on trade. His grand design of conquering Egypt, destroying British trade with the east and thereafter marching on India, was shattered by Nelson's destruction of the French fleet at Aboukir Bay in 1798. This British triumph was welcomed by all France's enemies and, with the help of subsidies, Pitt succeeded in forming a coalition of Austria, Russia and Turkey.

Napoleon's eastern ambitions had been thwarted. His army had been driven from Egypt and the Turks, with help from the Royal Navy, had stopped his advance into Syria at Acre. After abandoning his troops to fend for themselves, he returned to France with his reputation nevertheless enhanced by the glamour of his having taken the Pyramids and campaigned in the Holy Land. A new constitution was introduced in France and Napoleon became First Consul.

To explain how a battle came to take place in 1806 at the Val di Maida (Maida Vale) in the toe of Italy, some historical background is necessary. Naples and Sicily had been under Spanish Bourbon rulers since the sixteenth century, governed by viceroys until in 1734 they became a separate kingdom. King Ferdinand I of the Two Sicilies was III of Sicily and IV of Naples. He had come to the throne as a child when his father Charles inherited the Spanish crown. He came of age in 1767. A new English minister, William Hamilton, had arrived in Naples in 1764. He was to stay there for the rest of his career. Being patently trustworthy, he came to be a central figure in the court life of Naples and to know the king as well as anybody. Ferdinand's education had been woefully neglected. He had not

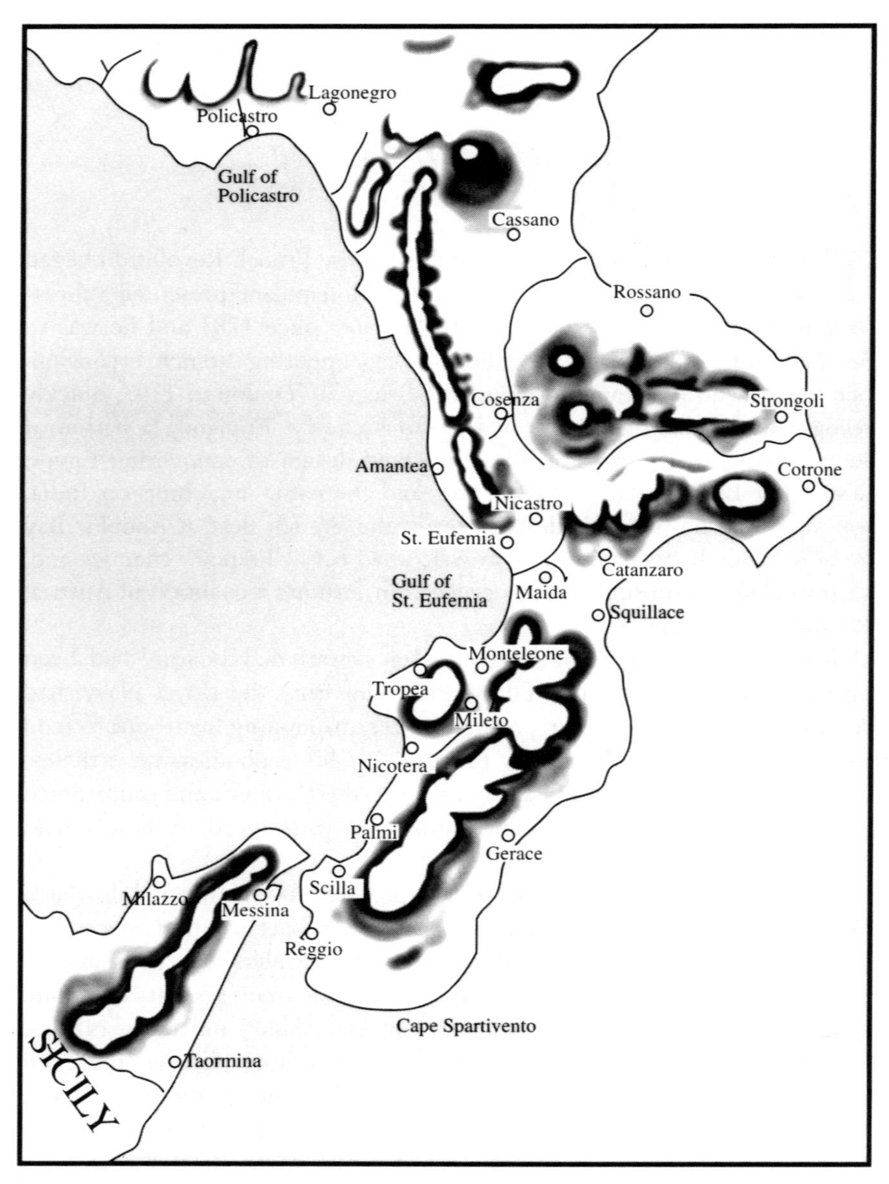
Lagonegro
Policastro
Gulf of
Policastro
Cassano
Rossano
Cosenza
Strongoli
Amantea
Cotrone
Nicastro
St. Eufemia
Catanzaro
Gulf of
St. Eufemia
Maida
Squillace
Monteleone
Tropea
Mileto
Nicotera
Palmi
Gerace
Scilla
Milazzo
Messina
Reggio
Cape Spartivento
SICILY
Taormina

Map 1: Italy

been made to study and as a child had done as he wanted. He was born with a passion for hunting. He spoke with the Neapolitan accent, the dialect of the lazzaroni, the lowest of Neapolitan classes, among whom he made his closest friends, regarding them as no more beneath him than all others. This democratic outlook made him popular all his life with the masses. His most striking feature was the large Bourbon nose which seemed to sprout straight from his forehead.

He married Maria-Carolina, the Empress Maria-Theresa's daughter, who was the older sister of Marie Antoinette. As a girl, she had shown herself wilful and impetuous, but she had been well instructed by her mother on her duties in this Hapsburg-Bourbon alliance. It was an age when dynasties were more important than nationalities. Under the marriage treaty, Maria-Carolina was to have a voice in the Neapolitan Council of State as soon as she had given birth to an heir. She soon did her duty amply in this way, and because of Ferdinand's distaste for business, she became the de facto ruler. She remained at heart an Austrian. In a letter to her brother, she described her husband as *'ein recht guter Narr'* (a right good fool).

When Nelson first visited Naples in 1793 as Captain of HMS *Agamnenon* he was warmly received at the court. Hamilton by this time was married to his young wife with whom Nelson became infatuated. Sir William Hamilton liked Ferdinand and sometimes accompanied him on hunting expeditions; Lady Hamilton was the Queen's most intimate friend. Under the Queen's influence, an Englishman, Sir John Acton, was the King's Prime Minister. Acton belonged to a Shropshire family and had been in the naval service of Tuscany. The Queen had persuaded her brother, the Grand Duke of Tuscany, to release him to reorganize the Neapolitan navy. The presence of an English Prime Minister at Naples not only removed the former ascendancy of Spain, it was also a boon for officers of the Royal Navy who were not linguists.

The pro-English sentiments of the court were not matched by performance. Nelson next visited Naples in 1798 when he was an admiral and fresh from the victory of the Nile. He was rapturously received but he had no illusions about the utter inadequacy of the Neapolitans to live up to their avowed intentions. They maintained diplomatic relations with France and the refitting of his damaged ships took an inordinate time. The difficulty for Naples was perhaps that the Austrians appeared to be half-hearted in prosecuting war against France. The Austrian General Mack was sent from

Vienna to command the Neapolitan army. When Nelson was taken to a review of the thirty thousand soldiers, what Mack called *'la plus belle armée d'Europe'*, Nelson politely said that the rank and file appeared healthy and good looking, privately noting that the force was 'with some few exceptions, wretchedly officerd'. It was agreed that four thousand infantry and six thousand cavalry should be landed at Leghorn in the enemy's rear to liberate the papal states so that with the advance of the Austrians from the north the French would be trapped. The Navy's part of the enterprise was carried out to perfection. Despite a strong gale, the Neapolitan troops were landed with their cannon and baggage and took possession of the town without opposition. But *'la plus belle armée'* soon evaporated. The Emperor of Austria had not marched and the French had driven back Mack's army taking all their baggage and artillery. Nelson's comment was: 'The Neapolitan officers have not lost much honour, for God knows that they had but little to lose, but they lost all they had.'

King Ferdinand had set out from Naples to join his army but he was soon among the soldiers disguised as civilians who made their way back to the city. According to one story, he discarded his uniform and put on the clothes of an aide-de-camp. Mack sent a dispatch reporting his army in full retreat and advising the King to leave before the French took possession of Naples. The Queen supposed that *'les scènes de Varennes avec toutes leurs suites'* were about to be enacted. In December the royal family with its entourage and the Hamiltons embarked in HMS *Vanguard* and Nelson transported them all to Palermo, the second capital.

The security of Sicily had for long been a major consideration for Nelson and his reason for his insistence on having a base for the Royal Navy at Malta. He saw Malta as 'the direct road to Sicily' which with its 500-mile coastline was particularly vulnerable. The defences of Sicily had been utterly neglected, in spite of the British subsidies which had been given for that very purpose. Nelson was not too blinded by his infatuation for Emma Hamilton to deplore 'the miserable conduct of this Court'. He had for long been waiting for some Neapolitan frigates which were never provided. The explanation for nothing having been done was that Austrian support could not be relied on if Naples were to take an actively belligerent part without first having been attacked by France: if Naples were to be attacked, the Emperor of Austria could be expected to come to the help of his brother-in-law. Nelson felt great relief when in

March 1799 Sir Charles Stuart arrived with two regiments from Malta to garrison Messina.

News from Naples was ghastly: it was a city divided against itself. The Regent left behind by the King had treated with the French for an armistice. A provisional government known as the Parthenopaean Republic had been set up under French protection. Some who had held court appointments had accepted office, perhaps in the hope of saving the country from anarchy. The mobs devoted to the dynasty had freed the prisoners and murdered any suspected of Jacobinism.

Then the tide began to turn. Austria having been attacked had some successes against the French. The Roman State and Southern Italy were in revolt; Russian and Turkish squadrons captured Corfu and the French in Naples found themselves in danger. A force of Calabrian peasants and brigands was formed by Cardinal Ruffo. He was joined by some Turks and Russians from across the Adriatic. The force totalled 17,000 and carried the Sicilian royal standard. By April, it was again flying from the islands in the Bay of Naples and at Castellammare.

Ruffo was an unusual sort of Cardinal. He had never been ordained but had been awarded his Cardinal's hat on retirement from the posts of Papal Treasurer-General and Minister of War. Nelson, who had for long disliked Ruffo whom he described as 'a swelled up priest', suspected him of trying to form a party hostile to the king's interests and was furious when he found flags of truce flying on the forts. The terms of the truce appeared to him to be a capitulation to the Neapolitan Jacobins. Those who had rebelled against their king were allowed to march out with their arms; those who did not wish to remain were to be evacuated to Toulon. The name of the king was not mentioned in the terms of the armistice. Nelson made plain that the armistice had been ended by the arrival of his fleet. No conditions except unconditional surrender were to be made with the Neapolitan Jacobins. He was prepared if necessary to arrest Ruffo and send him to Palermo and had been given authority by the king to do this if necessary. Capua and Gaeta, the last Jacobin strongholds in the kingdom, fell to Troubridge's seamen and marines. The way was cleared for the return of the Bourbon dynasty to Naples.

Further north in Europe, Napoleon's achievements had won for him a fervent supporter in the mad Czar Paul I who decided to withdraw Russia from the Coalition, leaving just Austria and England. Napoleon promptly attacked Austria and won his victory of Marengo in northern Italy; then he drove home his success at Hohenlinden in Bavaria. Austria sued for peace. The only course open to the French for defeating England appeared to be by blockade. Napoleon's new friend the Czar induced Denmark, Sweden and Prussia to join him in a League of Armed Neutrality for the protection of neutral rights, its object being to injure British trade. Before the League could become effective it collapsed, the Czar having been murdered and the Danish fleet put out of action by Nelson at Copenhagen.

The same year saw the end of Pitt's famous ministry, his resignation brought about by George III's refusal to agree to Catholic emancipation. Addington succeeded Pitt as Prime Minister and the short-lived Peace of Amiens was made in 1802.

Chapter Two

The Third Coalition

Under another change in the French constitution Napoleon was made Emperor. His foreign policy aroused great apprehension in England. Pitt became Prime Minister again in 1804 and he succeeded in forming the Third Coalition – England, Austria, Russia and Sweden on the one hand, France and Spain on the other.

Napoleon gathered an army of 210,000 men in camps along the Channel coast with a view to the invasion of England. At the same time, there were fears that Napoleon had new designs in the east. The strategy which Pitt wished the Third Coalition to follow was for the Prussians to advance in Holland, the Austrians and Russians in central Europe, leaving the British and Russians to attack the French in southern Europe. The peace of Amiens had provided for Malta to be restored to the Knights of St John but the British had not evacuated it and in March 1805 General Sir James Craig was ordered to the Mediterranean with instructions to co-operate with the Russians. Craig had been commanding the anti-invasion army in Essex. The French fleet managed to slip out of Toulon. As soon as Napoleon learned that Admiral Villeneuve had led it back into Cadiz, he gave up his earlier hope of invading England. Craig waited at Gibraltar where he received instructions from London to proceed to Naples and submit himself to the Russian general, his expeditionary force meanwhile assembling at Malta. Craig went ahead where he met General Maurice de Lacey of Grodno and his Quartermaster-General Oppermann. They had been living at Naples as civilians and Lacey had been ordered by the Czar to take command of the Russians and the British when the armies arrived. He belonged to a Limerick family whose men had left Ireland with the Wild Geese. One had become a field marshal in the Russian service at the time of Peter the Great. Lacey had a good reputation as a fighter but by this time he was an old man. He retained a strong Irish brogue. Oppermann was an Alsatian emigré, uncouth and mediocre. Unlike Sir James Craig who paid for all that the Neapolitans provided, the Russians insisted on all their expenses being met by the King. The King, mindful of Mack, was cynical about foreign generals in whom the Queen put her trust. When Lacey was presented to him he muttered loud enough for some courtiers to hear the Neapolitan word for 'donkey'.

It soon became obvious to Craig that the Russians had little understanding of amphibious operations. The land forces in the Mediterranean consisted of about 15,000 French in Apulia, 10,000 Russians at Corfu and the British, augmented now by Craig's reinforcements, about 10,000 at Malta. Lacey's suggestion was that the Russian troops should land at Naples when the Austrians took the field and that the British should distract the French army in Apulia under St-Cyr by landing in the Gulf of Taranto. Craig explained that after mid-September heavy surf made landings slow and that transports could not lie in safety off exposed coasts. Lacey gave way and it was agreed that the two armies should land simultaneously at Naples. The plan was that they should move northward to act upon the flank of the French army which was to be attacked on its front by the Austrians and Russians.

The British expeditionary force, about 8,000 strong, embarked at Malta and was joined at sea by the Russian force of about 14,000. It was known that Nelson was searching for Villeneuve somewhere in the Atlantic. News of Trafalgar did not reach Naples until shortly after the two armies had landed, on 21 November, the Russians at Baia and the British at Castellammare. The scale of the victory of Trafalgar was so great, the combined fleets of France and Spain – 33 ships – being defeated by Nelson's fleet of 27 ships, that it temporarily eclipsed the bad news from the north where Mack had surrendered the Austrian army to Napoleon at Ulm. On 30 November the King and Queen of the Two Sicilies reviewed the British army at Castellammare. The troops presented a superb spectacle and they fired volleys in honour of Trafalgar. Their bearing and discipline were the fruit of many months of hard training on the south coast of England against the threat of cross-Channel invasion and continued later in Malta. Sir John Stuart, second-in-command to Sir James Craig, commanded the parade. Acland commanded the 1st Brigade, Lowry Cole the 2nd and Brodrick the reserve. The royal carriage in which the Queen travelled was most dilapidated and drawn by six miserable horses tied together with ropes, 'very ill representing, to our English eyes, the eight proud cream-coloured Hanovarians and the gilded trappings which attach them to the splendid vehicle of our own Sovereign.'

King Ferdinand, the Hereditary Prince and young Prince Leopold arrived on horseback. The last was a manly little fellow. He had been caught trying to run away to sea when Nelson was in Naples. He was now dressed like a field marshal and doffed his hat with style each time the officers saluted. After the review, Queen Maria-Carolina was extravagant in her praise to Sir John Stuart. She had long been familiar, she told him, with the great qualities of the British sailor; now she could see that the British soldier was his equal in merit. The Italian noblesse kept exclaiming, *'Che belli soldati!'* and a few days afterwards a donation in money was sent to the army which when divided amounted to sixpence to each officer and man, a present from His Majesty of Naples.

By chance it happened that a spectator of the review was an Englishman whose fame would long outlive that of any of the soldiers – Samuel Taylor Coleridge. Coleridge had travelled to the Mediterranean for his health in 1804 and when in Malta had become secretary to the Governor, Sir Alexander Ball. He was making the return journey home via Naples where Sir Alexander Ball had promised to 'use his best interest with Mr Elliot, our Ambassador at Naples' to send him home with dispatches – which of course 'would frank him home'. As the royal party was leaving the parade ground, the setting sun blazed upon the brass plates and steel muskets of the soldiers, which Coleridge called 'a beautiful accident'.

The armies set out northwards, the British by the Terracina road, camping by the river Garigliano where they had communications on their right with the Russians whose headquarters were at Teano. The Neapolitan forces of some 25,000 men occupied Abruzzo and the road beside the Adriatic. The armies were about to advance when news arrived simultaneously of Austerlitz fought on 2 December and of the Treaty of Pressburg signed on the 26th of the same month. Napoleon had been infuriated by the perfidy of Maria-Carolina in allowing the allies to land in Naples bay in breach of a treaty of neutrality entered into by King Ferdinand – a treaty which the king tried to make the Russian ambassador believe had been extorted from him by force. He granted the Czar's wish to allow the Russian armies to retreat unmolested on the understanding that they would evacuate all the territory they occupied outside Russia. As regards Naples, Napoleon issued a proclamation affixed to the Treaty of Pressburg announcing that the 'Neapolian dynasty had ceased to reign . . . General St Cyr is advancing by forced marches to punish the treason of the Queen, and to precipitate from the throne this culpable woman who has violated in so shameless a manner all that is sacred among men . . .' His brother Joseph Bonaparte was appointed King of Naples.

Craig had no instructions about what he should do in such circumstances. One of his chief handicaps was the lack of communications. The only information from elsewhere which reached Naples was from French sources. In conditions of good visibility, the French could send signals between the Italian coast and mainland France with remarkable speed. The only means of communication available to Craig were frigates of which there were never enough. His last instructions from London had been written in April when his discretion to occupy Messina, which had been a possible course of action in his original instructions, had been withdrawn. The April instructions were confined to telling him to place himself at the disposal of General Lacey. Now the Russians were ordered to leave, bound for Corfu and the Black Sea. Craig explained to Lacey that his was an independent command.

Venice, Dalmatia and the former Venetian possessions on the eastern seaboard of the Adriatic had been ceded by Austria to France. Craig saw that the French could not fail to over-run the whole of Italy. British interests required the safe-guarding of Sicily with its long coastline from possible use by the French and Spanish ships which remained bottled up in Toulon and Cartaghena thanks only to the ceaseless vigilance of the Royal Navy. Yet still Maria-Carolina clung to the hope that Naples might return to being regarded by Napoleon as neutral; Cardinal Ruffo was sent on a mission to negotiate with the French. Craig was an upright man and was shocked by the Queen's perfidy. He had no doubt that if Napoleon granted a truce with Naples his condition would be a French garrison in Sicily. (His suspicions were later proved to have been well-founded: the Neapolitan ambassador in Paris had been authorised to promise to the French the exclusion from Sicilian ports of British shipping.) The Queen was the decision-maker in the Neapolitan court and she could exert formidable influence. 'Who could withstand the request of such a Queen?' Nelson had written. It is hard to understand now how even a level-headed man such as the Honourable Hugh Elliot, Sir William Hamilton's successor as British minister, could have taken the Queen's side in protesting to Craig against his determination to withdraw his army to Sicily. Elliot offered his services in negotiating with the French to halt their advance short of Naples. Craig was criticized from all sides. A soldier's morale is naturally impaired by retreating and there had been some criticism among some officers of his decision to withdraw south without having made contact with an enemy and now some disagreed with the plan to move to Sicily. The commander of the Neapolitan army, a French emigré, Count Roger de Damas, called Craig 'an insurmountable barrier to every kind of enterprise'. Craig remained firm, writing to Elliot: 'You seem to regard solely the benefit of the King of Naples while I am nevertheless anxious that no detriment shall arise to the interests of our country.' Taking the responsibility for acting in opposition to the minister's remonstrances, Craig sailed with his army for Messina.

How right he had been was soon apparent. The French marched on relentlessly, the fortress of Gaeta, on the coast about 50 miles north of Naples, left as the only stronghold being defended. King Ferdinand embarked on the one Neapolitan line-of-battle ship and sailed for his other capital, Palermo. Still the Queen did not give up hope of stopping the French before they reached Naples. Furious with the Allies, specially the English, she sent to Rome to offer the French the possession of Gaeta if they would halt and await the outcome of her further negotiations in Paris. When it became clear that only an unconditional surrender of the whole kingdom was what Napoleon demanded and that French troops on 9 February 1806 had actually crossed the frontier, she embarked and sailed for Palermo. On 16 February Craig received royal permission to occupy Messina, the troops having had to remain in their transports in the harbour for a fortnight.

To the simple soldier, the Queen's behaviour reeked of turpitude, yet she believed herself to have been a consistent supporter of the allied cause since 1792 when she had sent Neapolitan ships to Toulon to fight against the revolutionaries. She had allowed Nelson's fleet to revictual on its way to Egypt. She blamed the British for having broken the treaty of Amiens by not evacuating Malta and for having raised the Union flag there. (The Kingdom of the Two Sicilies had claimed a notional sovereignty over Malta.) She now feared that the British would occupy Sicily and reduce it to a British province. As she wrote to Damas, her most trusted adviser now that she had turned against Sir John Acton, 'I am entirely disanglomanized.'

A Council of Regency had been left at Naples and surrendered the kingdom to Masséna and Joseph Bonaparte. Count Damas, who had been mistrusted by Craig as 'of little worth as a military commander', retreated south with his troops into Calabria. He received no popular support, even the clergy preparing to welcome the French. Masséna despatched a division under General Reynier into the Calabrian mountains and he swiftly swept the Neapolitan army out of existence. The only exception was the garrison at Gaeta commanded by the Prince of Hesse-Philipstal who scorned to surrender to the French. On 25 February Reynier reached the Straits of Messina. Only the presence of Craig's little army prevented the French from crossing in the boats used by the Neapolitans.

Despite the British subsidies which had been paid for several years for the defence of the Kingdom of the Two Sicilies, the fortresses of Sicily were found to be neither armed nor provisioned. The Sicilian army was an ill-equipped force of about 6,000, adulterated with a demoralized rabble from Calabria. The militia consisted of a mere list of names. The Sicilian peasants were a hardy laborious race, good material for being organized by British officers if this were allowed. Many would gladly have served under the Union Jack – the name of King George was popular among them. Some were recruited to serve as seamen to man a small flotilla of oar-propelled gunboats which could operate in the Straits when sailing vessels were unable to. The Sicilians appeared to resent the Neapolitans, especially the corrupt and incompetent Court at Palermo. King Ferdinand himself was personally popular and when he visited Messina in March he received a rapturous welcome.

Early in 1806 Pitt died. He was succeeded as Prime Minister by Lord Grenville and the new ministry, which came to be known as the Ministry of all the Talents, took office in February. All its members were experienced: Spencer at the Home Office, Sidmouth Lord Privy Seal, Windham Secretary of State for War, Fox at the Foreign Office and Howick at the Admiralty. The problems were colossal. Trafalgar had removed any threat to British trade in the west but now that Russia had been defeated there was nothing to stop Napoleon in the east and Turkey lay open to attack. The Cabinet sent a warning to the Sicilian government saying that the British would not tolerate the admission of French troops to Sicilian ports and reaffirming authority to Craig to land his army in Sicily. Fortunately Craig had anticipated this by his brave independent decision. He must have been pleased when he read the remainder of his instructions in which he was assured 'of the most ample allowances for the difficulties of the situation in which you may have to act, and of the most indulgent construction of the motives by which you may be finally guided'.

Craig sent for reinforcements from both England and Malta. He had himself been a sick man before coming to the Mediterranean where he had hoped that his health would be restored. However, under the solitary burden of command it had again broken down. He left for home in April, Sir John Stuart taking his place.

Collingwood, Nelson's successor, detached two more ships of the line for the defence of Sicily and paid his first visit to the Court of Palermo. His reserved aloof manner was a complete contrast to Nelson's demonstrative nature. He was immune to flattery. He at once appreciated that the main threat to the security of Sicily was posed by the French and Spanish ships around Cadiz. The best defence of Sicily would therefore be to close the mouth of the Mediterranean. The Royal Navy did not have numerical superiority over the combined fleets of France and Spain. Its real strength lay in the inexperience of enemy crews and the moral effect on them of successive defeats. Collingwood hastened back westwards and off Cadiz he was joined by Sir Sidney Smith aboard the *Pompée*. With some misgiving on the part of Collingwood, Smith had been appointed to command the fleet in the central Mediterranean.

Chapter Three

Dramatis Personae

Sir Sidney Smith was a remarkable man who had already had a most colourful career. His name had become known to Napoleon at the time of the revolutionaries' capture of Marseilles when Smith had succeeded in boarding and setting on fire numerous French vessels in the harbour. Napoleon vilified him as 'a fire-ship captain'. During a period of inactivity in the Royal Navy he had volunteered his services to the King of Sweden (Gustavus IV) and had commanded a Swedish fleet and been rewarded with the Swedish Knighthood of the Sword. Then he returned to inshore operations against French shipping until he was caught at the mouth of the Seine by the turn of the tide and was taken prisoner. He was kept captive in Paris but after two years managed to escape. In Paris he had heard talk of Napoleon's designs on Egypt and British trade in the Levant. After his escape, he had reported what he had heard to the Admiralty and had become personally known to several ministers. Lord Spencer, writing about him to Windham in 1794, said, 'He is certainly an odd eccentric man . . . Look upon him as a Fellow of the College of Physicians does upon a quack doctor.' He was a great talker who had an excellent opinion of himself but his bravery and initiative were undeniable. His finest achievement had been at Acre. He had helped the Turks organise the defence and with his ships' guns had compelled the French to lift the siege and retreat south, Napoleon abandoning his army.

The appointment of Smith to the Mediterranean had been arranged in 1805 and Nelson had intended that Smith's expertise on inshore operations should be used against Spanish harbours and communications. He had been busy planning attacks with rockets and fireships against invasion barges at Boulogne, a method of warfare looked on with misgiving by Barham who thought Smith lacking in judgment – 'It is much safer to employ our friend Sir Sidney under command than in command.' Collingwood too thought rockets and fireships 'unworthy of the English, for their operations chiefly affect laborious individuals who know nothing of war but its miseries.'

Sir Sidney Smith (courtesy of the National Maritime Museum, Greenwich)

Moreover, if the Spanish were irritated into retaliation the British would be particularly vulnerable at Gibraltar.

Trafalgar and the death of Nelson had altered the nature of Smith's appointment to the Mediterranean. No orders issued to him by the Admiralty appear to exist but he called on Pitt on 10 January 1806 at Marlborough where Pitt lay on his deathbed and he said that he received a personal briefing from Pitt to the effect that the object of the expedition was to restore to King Ferdinand the sovereignty of the Two Sicilies, especially the Kingdom of Naples. This was to be a closely guarded secret. Just before leaving England, Smith wrote to Windham, 'Surely Lord Nelson's death ought not to operate so very disadvantageously to us as to change our system into a simple and passive one of defence when active operations towards destroying the enemy's means of annoying us and our allies are so much more efficacious . . .'

Sir Sidney, aboard *Pompée*, joined Collingwood off Cadiz. Collingwood had little sympathy with any project for regaining Naples for King Ferdinand and his Queen, saying realistically that when they had possessed it with all its resources and allies it had been abandoned as untenable. His orders to Smith, written from HMS *Queen* off Cadiz on 26 March 1806, concerned the defence of Sicily and even provided for circumstances in which French troops might enter Sicily under treaty or promise from the King of Naples. They were to be 'expelled and driven out, notwithstanding any remonstrance which the King of Naples may make . . .' Smith was to act in counsel with Mr Elliot and in harmony with the army, 'maintaining with them a constant and confidential correspondence, they must be privy to your most secret movements . . .'

Smith's reply was written from '*Pompée*, at anchor off Scalea, May 24th 1806'. He reported that he had arrived at Palermo on 21 April and taken his squadron under command. He did not say that on presenting himself at the Court his charm had immediately made a favourable impression on their Majesties. He learned that the fortress of Gaeta was still holding out against Masséna's army although no supplies had been sent. It was commanded by the eccentric Prince of Hesse-Philipstal who had no intention of surrendering to the French. He had rejected out of hand the offer made to him by Craig at the time of the withdrawal of the British army from Naples to lend him a stiffening of British troops. When Smith at Palermo heard that the Prince, now four months later, was still defying Masséna he at once complied with the Queen's wishes to take help to Gaeta. This involved removing from the Arsenal all the warlike stores which the ships could transport. Elliot was away from Palermo and when the news of Smith's action reached the army headquarters at Messina it caused some consternation because the weapons in the Palermo Arsenal had been relied on for the defence of Sicily. The Admiral was of course pleased with himself for what he had done:

> . . . I had the inexpressible satisfaction of conveying the most essential articles to Gaeta, and of communicating to his serene highness the governor (on the breach battery which he never quits) the assurance of further support . . . Things wore a new aspect immediately on the arrival of the ammunition. The redoubled fire of the enemy with red-hot shot into the Mole (being answered with redoubled vigour) did not prevent the landing of everything we had brought, together with four of *Excellent's* lower-deck guns, to answer this galling fire, which bore directly on the landing-place. A second convoy, with the *Intrepid*, placed the garrison beyond the immediate want of anything essential; and the enemy . . . was reduced to the defensive . . . dreading one of those sorties which the Prince of Hesse had already shown him his garrison was equal to, and which was becoming a much safer operation, now that the flanking fire of eight Neapolitan gun-boats I had brought with me, in addition to four his highness had already used successfully, would cover it . . .

The Prince of Hesse-Philipstal was the only general under whom Neapolitan soldiers performed well. He was unsparingly active and unconquerably brave. The *Gentleman's Magazine* of 7 June 1806 has an item reporting him 'to be encountered by domestic as well as external enemies. He lately shot his valet who under suspicious circumstances rushed into his apartment at night, and in the fellow's pocket papers were found which proved that he was suborned by the French to murder his master. On another occasion he precipitated a lady from the works into the moat while she was in treasonable correspondence with the enemy.' At times he appeared half-crazy but the troops whom he ruled with a rod of iron adored him.

The Admiral thought he might relieve the pressure on Gaeta slightly by appearing to threaten Naples with his line-of-battle ships, *Pompée*, *Excellent*, *Athénienne*, *Intrepid* and *Eagle*. The French did withdraw some of their battering-train from Gaeta. Naples was illuminated in honour of the proclamation of Joseph Bonaparte as King of the Two Sicilies. Smith decided against bombarding the city, considering that the wretched inhabitants already had enough misfortune and that the restoration of the capital to its sovereign would be no gratification if it were found a heap of ruins. In any event, he did not have a large enough force to land and keep order. This consideration did not apply when he arrived off Capri. Its situation commanding the shipping route from the Bay of Naples made Capri a desirable possession. When the French commander declined to surrender, guns from both decks of the *Eagle* made a bombardment for one hour and the marines landed. They climbed up the narrow pass to the summit and Captain Stannus, commanding the marines from *Athénienne*, himself killed the French commandant. When his death was known, the French beat a parley and a capitulation was signed. The garrison was allowed to march out with every honour of war and pass over to Naples, its brave commander having been buried with due respect.

Sir Sidney Smith continued his offensive actions against French fortified positions and on the *Pompée* reaching Scalea he succeeded in taking the castle:

> Finding, on my landing, that the tower was tenable against any force the enemy could bring against me from the nearest garrison in a given time, I took post with the marines, and under cover of their position, by the extreme exertions of Lieutenant Carrol, Mr Ives, master, and the petty officers and boats' crews, the guns were conveyed to *Pompée*, with twenty-two barrels of powder.

Early in June 1806, Sir Sidney arrived at Messina. Collingwood in his orders to Smith had naturally written of General Sir James Craig as the army's commander-in-chief but Craig had left Sicily so it was Sir John Stuart who received the Admiral. Smith at once asked for Stuart's help in providing troops for making raids on the coast for the purpose of destroying coastal batteries and spiking their guns. This seemed too trivial an object to Stuart who suggested a more ambitious operation which might have a longer-term advantage. It was the conjunction of Sir Sidney Smith and Sir John Stuart in command which led to Maida – but it was Sir Sidney Smith's vanity and egoism which limited exploitation of the victory.

Stuart* had had a very active military service since he was commissioned as ensign in the 3rd Foot Guards in 1780 at the age of nineteen. He had fought in the war of American independence. He was in numerous actions in the Low Countries between 1793 and 1795. Then he had served as a Brigadier-General under Sir Charles Stuart in Portugal and had raised the Queen's German Regiment (97th Foot, disbanded in 1818) and had taken part in the capture of Minorca. He was in command of the German Brigade in the expedition to Egypt under General Sir Ralph Abercromby and played a distinguished part at the battle of Alexandria. He had been ordered to march to Aboukir when he heard unexpected firing behind him; 'acting upon his own responsibility, he expeditiously returned and came up gallantly and most opportunely in excellent order with his German Brigade.' His action was providential for the Black Watch and saved the situation of the Reserve Brigade which was commanded by Sir John Moore. Stuart next went on a political mission to Constantinople and on his return to England was promoted Major-General and put in command of the anti-invasion forces in Kent. In March 1805 he had accompanied General Craig to the Mediterranean.

Sir Sidney Smith and Sir John Stuart had met when both were in the 1801 campaign in Egypt. The fleet had naturally played an important part, not only in transporting the army but in bombardment of French positions. Where the soldiers were landed in Aboukir Bay, the desert was waterless. Sir Sidney Smith was in command of the seamen who were landed to assist the army and he advised the digging of wells in the sand where there were palm-trees, advice which was acted on successfully. Sir John Stuart had no personal liking for the maverick admiral, any more than had his fellow naval officers, but Sir Sidney's combatant spirit and penchant for in-shore operations gave Sir John an opportunity which might not have been open to him if Collingwood had been on the spot.

Ever since the army had arrived at Messina the Queen had hoped for a landing in Calabria to support the Calabrese who were believed to retain their loyalty to their throne. General Fox, who was Lieutenant-Governor at Gibraltar, had been appointed to succeed Craig as Commander-in-Chief

* Lineage of Sir John Stuart

Porto di Messina, Sicily (courtesy of The National Maritime Museum, Greenwich)

but he could not arrive in Sicily for several weeks. Stuart saw an opportunity for possible glory during the short interim of his command. The French had two armies in Calabria: in Upper Calabria General Verdier was believed to be fully occupied with civil disorder; General Reynier was in command in Lower Calabria. Masséna had wanted Reynier's army to return north to help in the siege of Gaeta and to await its fall before attempting the invasion of Sicily. Napoleon typically had no illusion about priorities: '*La Sicile est tout, et Gaeta n'est rien,*' and he urged his brother Joseph to lose no time in crossing the Straits of Messina. Stuart saw an attack by the British in Calabria as the best means of defence for Sicily. If he could land a force of 5,000 men between the two French armies the Calabrese might rise and Reynier be compelled to withdraw. Stuart reckoned that a battle against equal numbers was unlikely to be disastrous for the British whereas for Reynier, operating in a hostile countryside, anything other than a victory would be fatal. A British victory on the other hand could be followed by the destruction of the military stores which the French had been accumulating in Lower Calabria for the invasion of Sicily and the dismantling of the forts on the mainland opposite the island. Stuart was energetic in self-help. He obtained leave to raise a corps of 500 Sicilian Fencibles who wore British uniform and drew British pay. Strenuous training was continued: in one day's march three soldiers of the 61st Foot dropped dead from exhaustion. Sir John told the admiral of his intentions. Sir Sidney was enthusiastic about the prospect of some aggressive military action and made the impracticable suggestion that the expeditionary force should be split into two, one half to be disembarked on either side of Gaeta. Sir John explained his less ambitious operation, of course expecting Sir Sidney to keep him informed of plans for naval co-operation. However, Sir Sidney left for Palermo and did not communicate with Sir John until 25 June when he wrote: 'The King is delighted to hear of your being disposed, as you are, to activity. In a private audience he begged me to speak plainly on that head to him saying he had been led to believe your letters to others were in a different tone.'

What had really happened at Palermo was that Sir Sidney had been dazzled by his welcome at the Court. His enthusiasm and his personal charm had together ingratiated him with the Queen whose flattery had greatly magnified his natural vanity. The Queen thought she had found another Nelson and 'Schmidt', as she called him, listened sympathetically to her wildest projects for the recovery of Naples.

At Messina meanwhile no time had been lost. The transports were alongside and fully victualled. There was still no sign of Sir Sidney. A return showing the disposition of ships in the Mediterranean reported HMS *Aurora* as 'being employed in search of Sir Sidney Smith'. Fortunately Captain Fellowes, the senior naval officer at Messina, was most zealous in providing all the naval co-operation the General asked for. There is an eye-witness account of the next stage:

> All the arrangements being complete and the fleet ready to sail, Sir John Stuart, in order to gain the advance of it, drove with one A. D. C. in his barouche to the point of Faro, and then embarked in a ship of war on the evening of 30th of June 1806. We were watching him from our quarters opposite when he stepped into his barouche. Never man, I thought, seemed better pleased with what he was about, or looked more to personate the spirit of enterprise. A nice military figure, he jumped gaily into his carriage, laughing with his aide-de-camp, and nodding kindly, drolly and significantly to the vivaing Messinese, who, notwithstanding the profoundest secrecy, had a pretty good guess what he was after, and rapidly drove off.

Chapter Four

Sources, and arrival of a new regiment

The eye-witness quoted at the end of the last chapter was Charles Boothby, a Royal Engineer officer who was aged twenty at the time he was writing about. The story in this book is mainly a compilation of the reminiscences of individuals who participated in the battle of Maida. They are listed in Appendix A.

A new regiment arrived in Sicily in May. This was the 2/78th (Second battalion Seaforth Highlanders, the Ross-shire Buffs). The regimental history by David Stewart of Garth who was a major aged thirty-four is graphic about the campaign. The battalion had been raised in 1804 when the 1st battalion was in India serving under Wellesley. The highland regiments had made themselves well liked by generals and Wellesley had asked for more. The officers of the new battalion were to raise men in accordance with rank: 100 men for a lieutenant-colonelcy, 90 for a majority, 50 for a company, 25 for a lieutenancy and 20 for an ensigncy; officers to take rank according to their dates of former commissions. Stewart was able to recruit 118 in his home area of Perthshire. The system of recruiting for rank worked well at this time and the men so recruited made splendid soldiers, attached and obedient to their officers. Stewart claimed that desertion was unknown and corporal punishment unnecessary. In the event of contemplated misbehaviour, the fear of a report reaching home was sufficient deterrent.

The new battalion assembled at Fort George and in 1805 was sent to Hythe where Sir John Moore had his well trained brigade of seasoned troops. The young soldiers of the 78th impressed Moore most favourably. Stewart told of an incident to illustrate the character of the regiment and of Moore:

> . . . Orders were issued for one field officer and four subalterns to join the 1st Battalion in India. The day before the field officer fixed on for

> this purpose left the regiment, the soldiers held conference with each other in the barracks, and, in the evening, several deputations were sent to him, entreating him, in the most earnest manner, to make applications either to be allowed to remain with them, or obtain permission for them to accompany him. He returned his acknowledgements for their attachment, and for their spirited offer; but as duty required his presence in India, while their services were at present confined to this country, they must, therefore, separate for some time. The next evening, when he went from the barracks to the town of Hythe, to take his seat in the coach for London, two-thirds of the soldiers, and officers in the same proportion, accompanied him, all of them complaining of being left behind. They so crowded round the coach as to impede its progress for a considerable time, till at last the guard was obliged to desire the coachman to force his way through them. Upon this the soldiers, who hung by the wheels, horses, harness and coach doors, gave way and allowed a passage. There was not a dry eye amongst the younger part of them. Such a scene as this happening to more than 600 men, and in the streets of a town, could not pass unnoticed, and was quickly reported to General Moore, whose mind was always alive to the advantages of mutual confidence and esteem between officers and soldiers. The circumstance was quite suited to his chivalrous mind. He laid the case before the Commander-in-Chief; and his Royal Highness, with the high feeling which he has always shown when a case has been properly represented, ordered that at present there should be no separation, and that the field officer should return to the battalion in which he had so many friends ready to follow him to the cannon's mouth, and when brought in front of an enemy, either to compel them to fly, or perish in the field.

What Stewart omitted to say was that the field officer in the story had been himself.

The training at Hythe was under the immediate direction of Moore. He began by instructing the officers and non-commissioned officers in 'the first principles of regular and connected movements, and in the firelock exercises'. When they had really digested the lessons they were sent to teach the soldiers, those slow in learning remaining in the ranks with the soldiers, not quitting them till thoroughly proficient and capable of teaching others. Moore was himself indefatigable, 'going from squad to squad giving directions and often forming the men in positions with his own hands'. To Stewart's regret at the time, the regiment was removed too early from

Moore's brigade. All the soldiers were Gaelic speakers, some with insufficient knowledge of English to understand the drill instructions.

Towards the end of 1805 the regiment sailed to Gibraltar, the convoy on its way passing through some of the floating wreckage left by the battle of Trafalgar. In May 1806 it was ordered to Sicily. Boothby wrote:

> On the 25th May our force received a valuable acquisition by the arrival of the 78th Regiment of Highlanders, a beautiful regiment, 900 strong, whose picturesque national dress made a great impression upon the Sicilians, though the women seemed to think it due to their modesty to say the dress was very ugly – 'and a very curious dress, and a very curious thing that such a dress should be approved of in England, a cold country'.

The reception of the highlanders by the younger and less genteel Sicilians had been rapturous to such a degree that the Archbishop protested about kilts to the General who replied evasively. David Stewart sensed that Sir John Stuart had been hoping for the 42nd (which he knew) and was disappointed to receive a new regiment, of which 600 men were under-age.

Chapter Five

Invasion

The expeditionary force which set out from Sicily was organized into four nominal brigades. The British order of battle is at Appendix B. Major General Sir John Stuart was in command; the Deputy Quarter-master-General was Lieutenant Colonel Henry Bunbury. The brigade commanders were Brigadier General Lowry Cole, Brigadier General Acland, Lieutenant Colonel Oswald and Lieutenant Colonel Kempt.

In the autumn of 1805 in Malta Craig had organized provisional battalions by removing from each regiment in his command its two flank companies and forming from them a Grenadier Battalion and a Light Battalion. Although no longer armed with grenades, the name 'grenadier' had been retained in infantry regiments for the right company of the line. It was usually composed of men of above average height. This system of composite battalions was thought to result in great pride and competition amongst the several companies to keep up the credit of their parent regiments. In addition, Craig had introduced a scheme of picking out the best shots from the remaining battalion companies as 'flankers'. The 'flanker' companies, each commanded by a subaltern, formed up in rear of their respective battalions and were used as skirmishers to cover the front or the flanks as required.

Craig's innovation was discontinued after a couple of years. Moore deplored the system on the grounds that a battalion already skimmed of its Grenadier and Light companies was left unacceptably weak. Yet it must be conceded that at Maida a brigade composed entirely of marksmen skilled in the use of Brown Bess was a winning factor, the British musket being a more deadly weapon than the French one, firing a ball of one ounce weight – 16 to the lb. against 22 to the lb. of the French musket.

The 1st Brigade was commanded by Cole and consisted of the Grenadier Battalion and the 27th, less its Light and 'flanker' companies. The 27th (Inniskillings) was Cole's family regiment and he had assumed command of it in Malta. The 2nd Brigade was commanded by Acland and comprised the whole of the 2/78th, and the 81st, less its Light and Grenadier companies. The 2/78th, having arrived in the Mediterranean too late to suffer dismemberment, was the only regiment at Maida to fight as a complete battalion.

The Light Brigade was commanded by Kempt, 81st Regiment, and was composed of the Light and 'flanker' companies of seven regiments, three battalion companies of the 35th, two companies of Corsican Rangers and one company of Royal Sicilian Volunteers.*

The Reserve Brigade, commanded by Oswald, consisted of sixteen companies from the 58th and De Watteville's Swiss.

There had not been sufficient transport to bring the 20th Light Dragoons; a detachment of just twenty were brought for mounted orderlies, the only other horses being the field officers' chargers. There were mules for the guns and baggage. The artillery consisted of ten 4-pounders, four 6-pounders and two howitzers. There was a small Royal Engineer detachment and each regiment had on its establishment one surgeon with two assistants. The total strength of the expeditionary force amounted to 5790. The 20th Foot, less its Grenadier and Light companies, had an independent role.

The French army under Gènéral Ebenezer Reynier was organized in three brigades (see Appendix C) and had a battery of horse artillery. They also had a cavalry regiment. Their total strength amounted to 7200.

Sir John Stuart's aim had been to strike at the narrowest piece of the Calabrian peninsula with a view to cutting Reynier's army into two before all the units which Reynier necessarily had to have on detachment in an occupied country could be brought together. His intelligence about the distribution of the French was found to have been wrong, the French forces having been less scattered than had been supposed. This did not become known until after the British landing had been successfully made in the Gulf of St Eufemia. In the absence of Sir Sidney Smith, the transports were taken under convoy of Captain Brenton and arrived in the Gulf on the night of 30 June. The advance brigade rendezvoused under the stern of HMS *Apollo*. A small picquet of French troops was seen on the shore

* The British Army at Maida

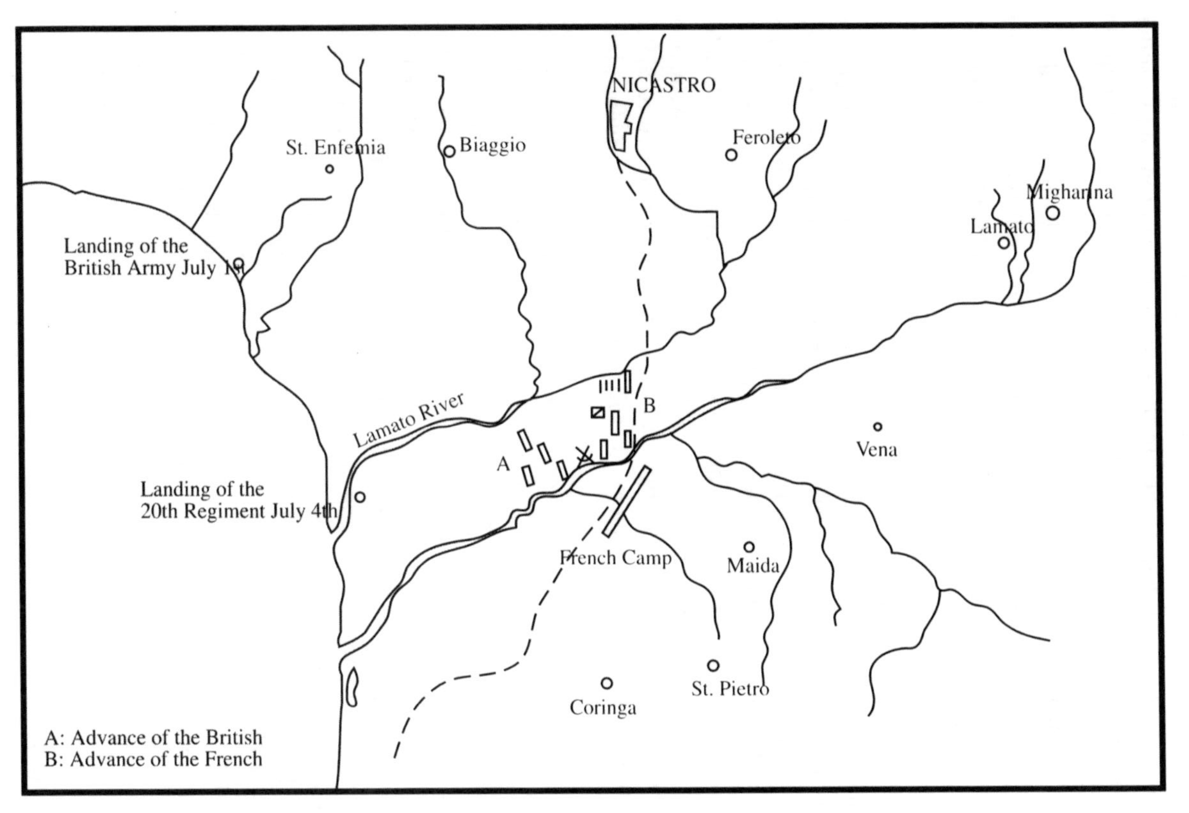

Map 2: Plan of the Battle

Bastione di Malta (1993)

and they immediately retired into the woods. Some armed Calabrese rowed out to the ships, with the assurance that there were few of the enemy in the neighbourhood. At dawn, the signal was given and the boats rowed rapidly towards the shore. The first landing took place in heavy rain; it should have been made by Colonel Kempt with the light infantry but the transport with his troops had not arrived, so Colonel Oswald led the disembarkation with the Corsican Rangers. They landed near an old tower named the Bastione di Malta and the boats returned to the transport for the Light Battalion and the 78th. As soon as Oswald saw that the second landing party was on its way, he advanced through the trees in the direction of the village of St Eufemia. They were met by a brisk fire and a company of the Corsican Rangers were charged and driven back by a superior number of the enemy. By then, the second landing had been successfully made and Oswald resumed the forward advance and charged the defenders on both sides, taking about eighty men and two captains prisoner and leaving thirty dead. The only British casualty was one sergeant of light infantry wounded. The enemy proved to have been mainly Polish troops with some French.

They had missed their opportunity by not attacking when the invaders were struggling through the surf.

Sir John Stuart issued a proclamation calling on the Calabrians to repair to his standard. Few appeared in arms. The Calabrese were a hardy and warlike race and had some traits of the highlander but their great difference to the Scottish highlander was that they had no attachment to their chiefs, who were nobles residing at the Court, unknown to their people except through the exactions of their agents. Not receiving the support he had expected and no word of any more distant help likely, Stuart began to hesitate whether or not he should re-embark his troops. Meanwhile the greater part of the army had advanced inland, some units as far as Nicastro, a hill-town on the north side of the valley opposite Maida, and had taken up a position between St Eufemia and Nicastro. The Bastione di Malta was made use of as a depot for the commissariat, the engineers building lines of defence with sandbags round it as protection for re-embarkation in the event of withdrawal. The landing of horses, mules, provisions and reserve ammunition continued throughout 2 and 3 July, a slow business on account of the surf. The strong wind required the transports to anchor at an inconvenient distance from a lee shore. When all was landed, the transports were sent back to Messina for the cavalry.

In the morning of the 3rd, information was received that General Reynier had pitched his camp near the village of San Pietro di Maida, a village about a mile below the hill-town of Maida. The size of the forces with him was not precisely known: estimates varied between 3,000 and 6,000 men. He was believed to be waiting there for the arrival of troops which had been on detachment further south. Sir John Stuart with a few staff officers and an escort of a grenadier company made a reconnaissance and from a piece of rising ground they were able to see the French camp on a hill overlooking the plain. Its position appeared to be a strong one. He then reconnoitred the ground in the outskirts of the woods to the south of St Eufemia. The Lamato river flowed from near the French camp to the sea about eight miles from where the British had landed. The valley was broad and level at its centre but bounded on both sides by high and steep hills covered by woods, the gentler slopes within the valley showing fields of ripening corn. Sir John Stuart judged that the left of the French front would be its most vulnerable place. Despite his lack of cavalry, he decided to lose no time and gave orders for recalling the units which had advanced to Nicastro and for the troops to set out to march along the edge of the bay. Stuart thought speed important because he believed that Reynier was still waiting for more troops.

It was learnt later that Reynier had himself been reconnoitring on the afternoon of 3 July and both generals had been in the wood near St Eufemia at about the same time. Reynier's forces were less scattered than had been supposed. Seven of his ten battalions had been in the toe of the peninsula. When he heard of the British landing he at once moved north, not wanting to be cut off from General Verdier's troops in Upper Calabria. 'Five thousand men were enough to thrust 6,000 or 7,000 English into the water,' he boasted. Leaving detachments at Reggio and at the castle of Scilla, he marched with over 4,000 men from the 1st Léger and 42nd Ligne and two squadrons of cavalry along the coast road to Maida. At Palmi he had been joined by 630 men of his Swiss regiment. This Swiss battalion was by coincidence also De Watteville's. Its colonel was a cousin of the well-trusted Louis de Watteville who commanded the British Swiss regiment. At Monteleone his force was joined by a second chasseur squadron which had ridden across the peninsula from Catanzaro. Only one Polish battalion remained in the north with detachments to keep his communications open. It was troops from this battalion which had brushed with the invaders. Now Reynier had with him a fighting force of 6,440. It was an achievement in the Napoleonic tradition to have assembled an army and reached Maida – 80 miles away from Reggio – in only three days.

Chapter Six

The Battle

The army marched in parallel columns, Kempt's brigade on the inland side in front, Cole behind him. Acland's brigade was in front on the seaward side, with Oswald in his rear. Each brigade had two light mountain guns carried by mules; three heavier guns were pulled behind Acland's brigade. The baggage mules with Kempt's brigade took fright at something as they were going through a wood and in panic galloped back, the cooking utensils with which they were loaded clattering loudly, and when someone shouted, 'It's the French cavalry,' there was much confusion and some Grenadiers scattered into the trees. Lieutenant Colonel O'Callaghan, the battalion commander, was furious and remained sensitive to any mention of camp kettles. The march was most fatiguing, especially for those who had been recalled from Nicastro. The column nearest the sea had to shuffle along in shingle and the men inland were in marshy pastureland and scrub, mainly myrtle bushes. The myrtles were in flower and many soldiers picked a sprig. At the Lamato estuary they were ankle-deep in black slime. Progress was slow and the field-guns were transported only with great difficulty. The column was protected by the *Apollo* and two other frigates at sea with their guns ready to come into action if required. At 7 a.m. the march was halted and Sir John with his staff went to reconnoitre. The French could be seen in a very strong position on a wooded hill. Attacking their left flank would mean a further march, then crossing the Lamato and finally climbing the hill whose scattered trees and bushes would make it defendable foot by foot. The reconnaissance party suddenly saw to their astonishment the French troops leave their advantageous position, beginning to come down into the plain. This was quite unexpected. The July day had brought an early heat haze and nothing had been observable from the line of march. Parties of French cavalry which had been seen riding parallel to the left flank of the column had been thought perhaps to be a screen to hide a withdrawal. In fact, Reynier had been intending all the time to attack. His cavalry scouts had given him exact information about British dispositions and he had deliberately waited until his enemy should be far enough from the sea and outside the protection of naval guns before a clash between the two armies could occur.

At 8 a.m. the British army wheeled inland and at a quarter to nine General Reynier 'descended upon his adversary', as he said in his dispatch, intending 'to make a vigorous charge, which should smash up a section of the enemy's force, so that the remainder would not be able to re-embark, and would have to surrender.' Having turned east away from the sea the British army was now in echelon of brigades with Kempt's Light Brigade the furthest forward on the right. Next was Acland, and on the extreme left Cole: Oswald with the reserve a little behind and in the centre. The French were similarly in echelon, but from their left, so that the left of their front and the right of the British front were closer than the remainder of the two lines. The distance between the two armies was at first about three miles but rapidly grew less. Reapers in the cornfields eagerly pointed out the advance of the enemy when they were only about a mile away. The French guns opened fire but most of the shots passed over the British first line with little effect.

David Stewart's account cannot be bettered:

> Two armies in parallel lines, in march towards each other, on a smooth and clear plain, and in dead silence, only interrupted by the report of the enemy's guns; it was more like a chosen field fixed upon by a general officer for exercise . . . than a real battle. No two rival commanders could ever wish for a finer field, for a trial of the courage and firmness of their respective combatants; and as there were some present who recollected the contempt with which General Reynier, in his account of the Egyptian expedition, had chosen to treat the British, there was as much feeling mixed up with the usual incitements, as, perhaps, in any modern engagement . . . To the young Highlanders, of whom nearly 600 were under age, the officers, with very few exceptions, being equally young, and inexperienced, it was a critical moment. If we consider a formidable line, which, from numbers, greatly outflanked our first line, supported by an equally strong second line, the glancing of whose bayonets was seen over the heads of the first; the advance of so preponderating a force on the three regiments of the 1st Brigade, (the 2nd being considerably in the rear), was sufficiently trying, particularly for the young Highlanders. Much depended on the event of the first onset; if that were successful, their native

> courage would be animated, and would afterwards stand a more severe trial. In this mutual advance, the opposing troops were in full view of each other, which enabled our men to make their remarks on the marching, and on the manner in which the enemy advanced. They did not always preserve a correct steady line but sometimes allowed openings and intervals by careless marching; showing, as the soldiers observed, that they did not march as steadily as they themselves did. Additional circumstances inspired still greater confidence. I have already noticed that the enemy's guns were not well served and pointed too high: not so the British. When our artillery opened, under the direction of Major Lemoine and Captain Dougal Campbell, no practice could be more perfect. Every shot told and carried off a file of the enemy's line. When the shot struck the line, two or three files, on the right and left of the men thrown down, gave way, leaving a momentary opening before they recovered and closed up the vacancy. The inexperienced young Highlanders, believing that all the vacant spaces had been carried off, shouted with exultation at the evident superiority . . . The lines were fast closing, but with perfect regularity and firmness. They were now within three hundred yards distance, and a fire having commenced between the sharpshooters on the right, it was time to prepare for an immediate shock.

The columns coming down were composed of four battalions from two of the best French regiments, the 1st Léger and the 2nd Ligne, veteran troops with an old record of victory from Napoleon's first Italian campaigns. They amounted to 2,880 men.

As David Stewart wrote, fire had commenced on the right and in the interests of narrative it will be easier to describe the battle from right to left of the British line, each brigade being involved simultaneously in separate engagements. The fighting began on the right of the line because the French line of descent from their camp had wheeled on its left brigade, bringing the French left closer to the British right.

When Kempt saw the French advance he formed his Light Brigade into line and ordered his men, who had been encumbered with their canteens and greatcoats worn bandolier-wise, to ground arms and unburden themselves. The French, noticing their enemy halt, took it for hesitation. Kempt sent the Corsican and Sicilian sharpshooters out to his flank into the scrub on the left bank of the Lamato. The river-bed was almost dry and as they advanced they were attacked by two companies of French skirmishers placed

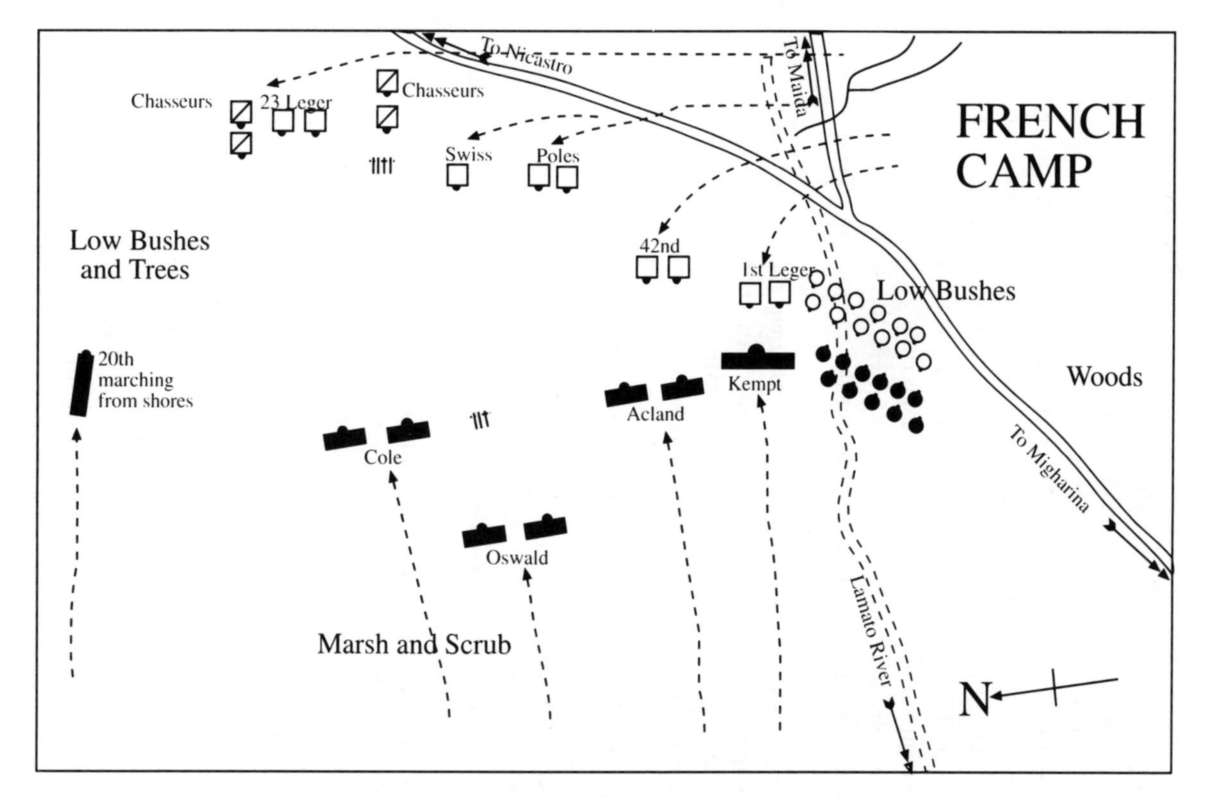

Map 3: The Battle

there by Compère to protect his left flank. The Corsicans, receiving a sudden volley, broke and fell back in some disorder. Kempt detached his two right companies, the light infantry company of the 20th and the 'flankers' of the 35th, who rallied the Corsicans and drove back the French into the wood. In this engagement, Captain McLean commanding the light company of the 20th was shot through the heart. He was the only British officer killed in the field. After their effective intervention, the 20th and 35th returned at the double to take their place on the right of the Light Battalion. They had just got back when the crash came. The 1st Léger in two battalion columns was coming at the right and centre of Kempt's line. The two French battalions had 1,600 men; the seven British companies had only 700. The skirmishers of both sides were occupied with each other on the far side of the Lamato.

The French were in two columns of 800 men each, drawn up in column of companies, i.e. with a front of some sixty men each, and a depth of fourteen. Each battalion had seven companies. The front of each column was about sixty yards. Kempt's men were in line, with trailed arms, two men deep, giving him a front of 350 yards. Every man in the British line was a picked marksman, all being Light company men, and all could aim at the front or flank of one of the two French columns. Only the men in the two front ranks of each column of the French, on the other hand, were able to use their muskets. This fact seemed of no importance to Compère who was riding with his staff between the two columns. He thought he was going to break through the British line by sheer impact, as he had broken through Austrians in Lombardy. The columns were certainly a formidable sight, advancing like rolling boulders in an avalanche. They were marching at full speed to lessen the time within musketry range, what Boothby called the '*pas de charge*', their commander exclaiming furiously as they advanced, '*Ne tirez pas! ne tirez pas! À la bayonette! à la bayonette!*' The trumpets were blaring and the men shouting, '*Vive l'Empéreur!*'. Kempt halted as the enemy drew near, shouting, 'Steady Light Infantry. Wait for the word. Let them come close.' Then, when the columns were within half-musket shot, 'Now fire!' The first volley at 150 yards laid low most of the first line but the rest still came on. The second tore into the heart of the disordered mass whose impetus still carried it forward. When the smoke from the third volley cleared, they saw bayonets at their chest and turned to flight.

A Calabrian who witnessed the fight from neighbouring high ground reminiscing afterwards thought as the French did that when the British troops halted they were going to retreat. But '*Santo diavoluni!* In the next instant after the halt there was a shout and a rushing forwards and then it was the French that were running away. They went down like grass before the mower.' Many of the French, still burdened with their knapsacks, were overtaken and slaughtered. Some of the Light Infantry took off their footgear, the better to charge through marshy ground; they were hunting the French like hounds until bugles sounded the recall.

Compère was severely wounded. A marksman from De Watteville's Light company had taken deliberate aim at him. According to Boothby, he had led the charge 'with an *acharnement* that seemed like individual hate, and on being taken he rode with his shattered arm through our ranks, menacing with the action of his other arm, and cursing and swearing with most voluble bitterness.' He thought he had been beaten because his men had flinched at the last moment.

Acland's brigade, being on the left and slightly behind Kempt's, came level with Kempt's at the same time as the French 42nd Ligne came up on the flank of the 1st Léger. At the same time as the French battalions received volleys from Acland's two regiments, Compère was suffering defeat. David Stewart wrote: 'The lines were fast closing, but with perfect regularity and firmness. They were now within three hundred yards distance . . . The enemy seemed to hesitate, halted, and fired a volley. Our line also halted, and instantly returned the salute, and when the men had reloaded, a second volley was thrown in. The precision with which these two volleys were fired, and their effect, were quite remarkable. When the clearing off of the smoke (there was hardly a breath of wind to dispel it) enabled us to see the French line, the breaks and vacancies caused by the men who had fallen by the fire appeared like a paling, of which parts had been thrown down or broken. On our side it was so different, that, glancing along the rear of my regiment, I counted only fourteen who had fallen from the enemy's fire. As soon as the smoke had cleared our line advanced at the charge and the 42nd Ligne withdrew swiftly but not in confusion. They halted just in front of their second line, a constant running fire being maintained, until they had reached a position about a mile away. Here they could support Reynier's right wing and cover his left if Kempt's Light Brigade should turn in on them instead of chasing the remnants of Compère's brigade.'

The French cavalry now tried to harass the 78th and 81st and Acland ordered them to form squares. 'Either from their horses not being properly broke, or, rather from the sharp running fire kept up in their faces,' wrote David Stewart, 'the dragoons could not, with all their exertions bring them to the charge.' Eventually they galloped round the flanks of their line to the rear, turned their horses loose, and fought on foot.

By contrast with his detailed account of the opening of the battle, David Stewart is not explicit about the fighting at close quarters. Doubtless modesty restrained him from saying much about his own part and he did not want any of the young regiment blamed for an understandable mistake. The second French line contained a Swiss regiment, their De Watteville's. The British De Watteville's was guarding the Bastione di Malta, only its Light company, in Kempt's brigade, being involved in the fighting. Now Acland's infantry saw advancing upon them from the second French line the De Watteville's in the French service. They were 'dressed in a kind of light claret coloured uniform, something like scarlet when much worn, and with hats so much resembling those of the band of our Watteville's, that, when the corps was seen advancing from their second line, the Highlanders, in their inexperience, believed they were our own, who had, in some manner, got to the front; and word was passed quickly to cease firing. The fire had accordingly slackened before the voice of the mounted officers whose elevated position enabled them to distinguish more clearly, could be heard, and the enemy, believing this relaxation to proceed from a different cause, advanced with additional boldness. This brought them so close, that when the men were undeceived and recommenced firing, it was with such effect that in 10 minutes the front was cleared . . .'* A fact which did not become generally known until much later is that it was David Stewart's promptness which saved the situation. He rallied the soldiers and led them forward in a charge which drove back the French centre. Lieutenant Colonel Patrick MacLeod commanding the 78th was struck in the chest by a musket ball and called to a sergeant to help support him in the saddle. Stewart was himself severely wounded, James Macdonell taking over command of the battalion. Stewart never fully recovered the use of a broken arm. Acland's

* The French regiment being mistaken for the British

brigade in its two successive victories over the 42nd Ligne and the foreign battalions suffered a heavier loss than any other part of the British army – more than half the total British loss at Maida.

The author of the article about Major-General David Stewart of Garth in the *Military History of Perthshire* (published 1908), recorded that 'to the day of his death, General Stewart, out of loyalty to the memory of the officers whose mistake had nearly lost the day, observed the greatest reticence on the subject of Maida.' However, a private memorandum about the battle was written by him on 12 July 1828, the year before his death, and a copy has survived among family papers.* The memorandum appears to be part of a memorial intended for submission to the King of the Two Sicilies, seeking 'some mark of distinction to the two surviving field officers, Major-General David Stewart and Colonel James Macdonell.' Stewart wrote that after the enemy had been driven back by the first charge, he saw that the officer commanding the 81st regiment appeared not to have understood his instructions, or was not carrying them out. He therefore rode over to him and 'a remedy was instantly applied'. On returning to his own regiment, he found that orders had been received to retreat. Stewart hurried off to the brigade commander and begged him to rescind the order. Acland answered that he had not given an order to retreat. Stewart rode back and found all but one company in close column ready to march off. He ordered them to face to the right about and to form line and to open fire – during this time the enemy had come within musket range. 'So correct and deadly was the aim of the young soldiers that in ten minutes the field in their front was cleared . . . Thus the misapprehension or mistake about orders turned out to be highly advantageous; and Major Stewart learned afterwards from a French officer that it was considered by them as an able manoeuvre or ruse . . .' According to a family legend, Stewart shot an officer. If this was true, the shot was certainly not fatal.

On the extreme left of the British front, Cole's brigade, consisting of the 27th and a composite battalion composed of the grenadier companies, reached the battlefield a quarter of an hour after Kempt and Acland had come into action. Major Roveara had been a spectator. 'The *coup d'oeil* was

* Memorandum left by Stewart of Garth 1828

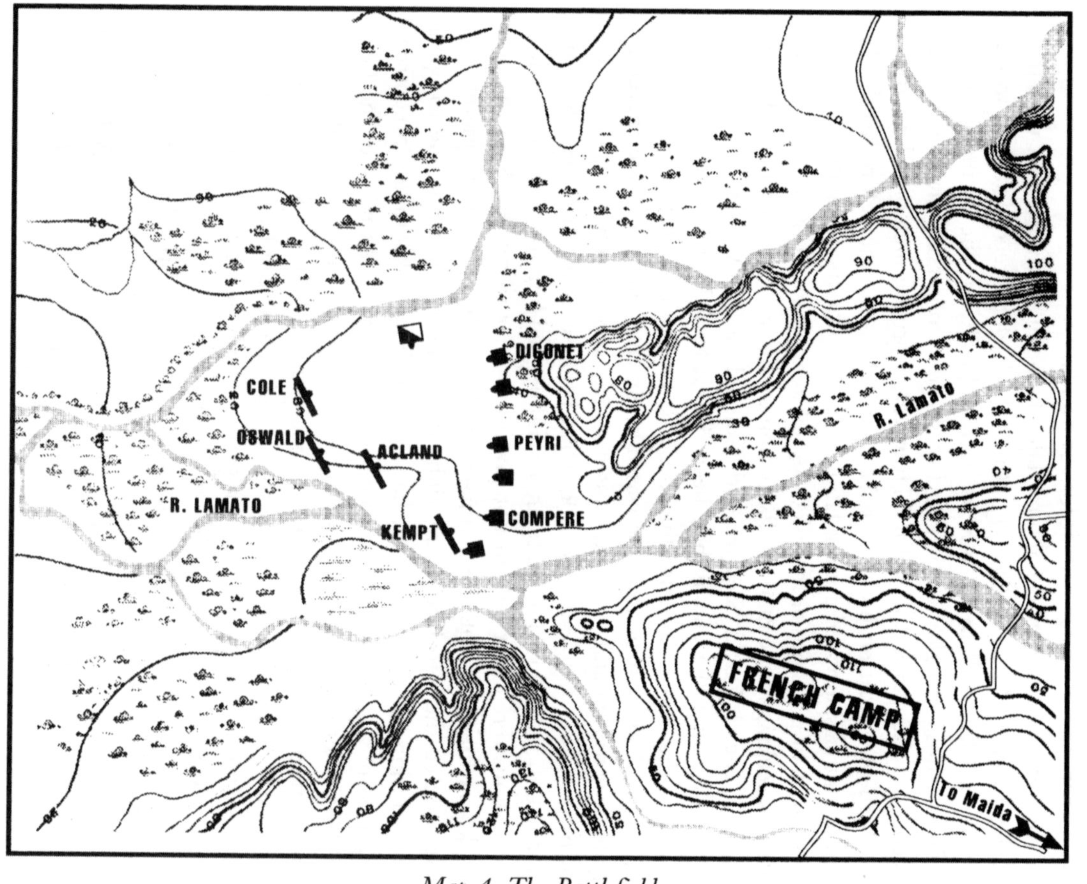

Map 4: The Battlefield

magnificent – our fine troops as steady and in as good order as on the parade ground, *vis-à-vis* the French, their arms glittering in the sun. I had never seen anything of the sort before and the sight struck me with admiration . . .' Shortly afterwards Roverea saw on his right the enemy, completely routed,

> flying in all directions, letting themselves be killed or taken prisoners, for they could not run as fast as our men who had thrown away their accoutrements. On the left, on our side the combat did not go so well for us, for some sharpshooters had come close enough to incommode us with their fire. While my General [Cole] was thinking that he ought not to allow some 'flankers' to dislodge them, a shell exploded quite close to us and set fire to the dried grass of the field in which we were, and very soon the whole was in flames, and this accident caused some confusion in the centre of the 27th Regiment. But the smoke prevented the enemy from perceiving this. At the same time a body of their cavalry advanced and threatened our left flank and appeared to be about to charge. So much so that our mounted officers drew sword or pistol and prepared to defend themselves in the mêlée. Two companies of grenadiers who were moved from the right of the brigade to reinforce the left, suffered very much. A mass of infantry advanced behind the cavalry and the moment became critical for us. General Cole threw back three companies of the 27th with two of the grenadiers, and still the enemy advanced . . .

Lieutenant Colonel O'Callaghan, riding along the front of the line which was bracing itself to receive a cavalry charge, kept vociferating, 'Grenadiers, remember the camp kettle mules, you damned rascals! Remember the camp kettle mules!'

Now came the dramatic finale. As was mentioned, the 20th, less its light company which had played a distinguished role in Kempt's brigade, had not sailed with the main part of the expeditionary force but had been cruising off the coast in order to deceive the French about the point of invasion. They had been in large open boats, each capable of holding about a hundred men but in fact with only one officer and about eighteen men in each boat: they were expected to hoodwink the French completely. They were a thoroughly well-trained and experienced regiment, under their commanding officer, Robert Ross. In Malta they had been repeatedly out on all-day training exercises across country in hot weather. Back at Messina, they embarked in transports on 3 July and were in the Bay of St Eufemia when they were signalled by Sir Sidney Smith who had just arrived there. The Admiral informed them that Sir John Stuart's attack was to take place that day and they landed on the coast two miles from the battlefield. Charles Steevens reminisced:

> Without waiting for orders, our gallant chief, Colonel Ross, gave directions for the regiment to disembark. We could hear the firing and see the smoke; we therefore cheerfully obeyed the order and landed forthwith, after filling our haversacks and canteens, for officers as well as men carried their three days' provisions, and their blankets and change of linen. In landing the boats had to go through a great deal of surf, and the men spoilt all their cartridges, but having some casks of ammunition in the boats, we soon replenished their pouches, and immediately hurried across the country, through woods and marshes, in the direction whence the music of cannon and musketry was heard . . .

Bunbury was expecting Oswald's brigade to move forward into the gap between Cole and Acland and he was trying to hasten the bringing up from the rear of more musket ammunition. He was riding along behind Cole's brigade, observing the French sharpshooters stealing further and further round Cole's left flank, when one of his staff officers came galloping up from the beach with the news that the 20th had landed and was coming through the brushwood at the double. Bunbury rode to meet them and explained to Ross

> how matters stood. He caught the spirit of the affair in an instant, pressed forward, drove the swarm of sharpshooters before him; gave the French cavalry such a volley as sent them off in confusion to the rear, and passing beyond the left of Cole's brigade, wheeled the 20th to their right and opened a shattering fire on the enemy's right. The effect was decisive.

Reynier had been utterly surprised by the sudden arrival of the 20th. He was unable to maintain his ground and drew off his troops, covering the retreat by sharpshooters and horse artillery. He left the plain and headed rapidly up the valley towards Catanzaro.

Chapter Seven

Victory

No account of the battle written now could omit quoting Bunbury's strictures of Sir John Stuart. As was noted in the article about Sir John Stuart in the *Dictionary of National Biography*, Bunbury had 'a strong antagonistic bias' towards Stuart. This is what he wrote:

> But where was Sir John Stuart? And what part did he play in this brilliant action? To say the truth, he seemed to be rather a spectator than the person most interested in the result of the conflict. He formed no plan; he declared no intention; and scarcely troubled himself to give a single order. Perfectly regardless of personal danger he was cantering about the field, indulging himself in little pleasantries, as was his wont. He launched forth with particular glee when a Sicilian Marchese, whom he had brought as an extra aide-de-camp, betook himself to shelter from fire behind a haystack. But after the charge of Kempt's light infantry and the utter rout of the French left wing, a change came over the spirit of Sir John. He still dawdled about, but broke into passionate exclamations: 'Begad, I never saw a thing so glorious as this! There was nothing in Egypt to equal it! It's the finest thing that I ever witnessed.' From that moment he was an altered man, full of visions of coming greatness; as I found that I could get no orders from him, I made it my own business to go round to the leaders of brigades, to give them the information they wanted.

In his dispatches Stuart was generous in his praise of Bunbury and there appears to be no explanation for the harshness of Bunbury's opinion. Stuart was never a popular general like Sir John Moore, who was the object of hero-worship to individuals of both genders. As soon as Boothby at the Bastione di Malta knew of the victory he was able to leave the entrenchments and canter to the scene of battle. It was

> still smoking with recent carnage, peopled with prostrate warriors distorted with the death agony, harnessed for battle in gay colours, feathers and gold, but stained and bathed in their own life-blood . . .

> The events of the battle were in some sort told by the mute and motionless, but sad and appalling forms with which the ground was covered . . . A picture of a battle represents but one instant; no figure can move, yet all seem stirring and tumultuous . . . The chieftain's hand is lifted to strike; his lips have not closed since the shout of victory or mandate of battle has passed through them. The passions, too, in the midst of death remain strongly impressed upon each warrior's features. The daring courage, the bitterness of anger or revenge, and the thrilling agony of mortal pain – all speak distinctly in the countenance of the dead.

When Boothby arrived the severely wounded, friend and foe without distinction, were being moved from the field. The British casualties had been astonishingly light. Only one officer was killed, Captain McLean of the 20th Light Company who had led his men in the successful counter-attack against the French sharpshooters on the left bank of the Lamato. The total British casualty list had been 327: 44 men killed; 13 officers and 269 men wounded. The French casualties, killed, wounded or prisoners, exceeded 2,000. The fighting which had begun at about nine o'clock was all over by eleven.

The weather had been insufferably hot and the discomfort of the soldiers in their red uniform was appalling. On arriving at the beach nearest the battle-field the troops, each brigade in turn, were given permission to bathe. While Cole's brigade, the extremely brawny grenadiers and Enniskillens, were in the sea, a staff officer came galloping in from the front, shouting out that the French cavalry were approaching. In a moment, the troops sprang to arms. Throwing their belts over their shoulders and grasping their muskets, they drew up in line without waiting to put on a stitch of clothing. The alarm had been quite groundless. The air was very hazy and the plain full of dust; a junior staff officer had had an imperfect view of a herd of stampeding buffaloes which he had mistaken for *chasseurs à cheval*.

Sir Sidney Smith in his flagship was anchored close to the shore. He landed to congratulate the general and invited him to spend the night on board *Pompée*. After some hesitation, Stuart accepted, taking Bunbury and his ADCs with him. There must have been considerable coolness between the two commanders, at least on Sir John Stuart's side. When Sir Sidney Smith had written announcing the royal decree which had appointed him Viceroy, he had said that he was bombarding Amantea, about 15 miles north of Eufemia Bay, as a diversion. In his reply, Sir John Stuart had begged the admiral not to distress potential friends by aggressive action and had acknowledged with dignity the news of Sir Sidney's viceregal appointment, saying that as he was himself commander-in-chief of a British army he did not consider himself under the orders of anyone other than his own king. He went on:

> 'As I gave you full and early intimation of my intended movements, I can only regret that I had not your personal presence with us at our début. From your representative, however, Captain Fellowes, and from every part of the Naval Department under his direction, I have met with the most zealous promptitude and ability in forwarding my views for the public service.'

Sir Sidney Smith now showed the general every honour. With disconcerting frankness, he informed his military guests that he had expected them to be defeated, in which event he had determined to run the *Apollo* frigate ashore, with her broadside to the beach to protect the retreat. After dinner, the two commanders demonstrated the Turkish way of arranging turbans and Sir John was invested with a shawl of honour after the oriental fashion. Sir Sidney's cabin was full of shawls. According to Sir John Stuart (but omitted by Bunbury), in discussing the future, he suggested that Sir Sidney Smith should cruise northwards since everything to the south was from the French point of view 'in the power of the enemy'.

At daybreak Sir John Stuart relanded. The army had formed a camp about a mile from the battlefield and near the sea. There were some tents for officers and the wounded were accommodated on board ship. Sir John Stuart marched his force to Maida. Some valuable equipage was found in the French camp. The general busied himself with composing his dispatch but first he wrote to his senior officer who had been left in Sicily:

> Calabria
>
> British Camp
> Maida fifth July 1806
>
> My dear Broadrick,
>
> I trouble you with a few lines to acquaint you with the satisfactory circumstances of our having yesterday attacked and completely defeated

General Reynier in a pitched battle on the plains of Maida. The enemy by all accounts consisted of at least seven thousand infantry and about three hundred cavalry with four six-pounders and two howitzers.

Their loss to our knowledge in killed wounded and prisoners is upwards of 2,000, as the Calabrese are hourly bringing in prisoners from the mountains I need not hesitate at adding another 1,000 to the number. It is impossible to detail all our gallant troops have merited. General Compair with many officers of rank are my prisoners. Had I had the few mounted 20th Light Dragoons from Messina with me not an individual would have escaped. I am happy that with all this our loss has been comparatively small – but one officer and 40 men killed, seven officers and about 250 men wounded. Capt. McLean 20th Lt. Comp. unfortunately fell but Colonel Ross with the 20th Regt. landed during the action at a moment to render us a most essential and critical service.

Yrs. most faithfully,

J. Stuart
Major General

Reynier has gone off with his broken remains towards Catanzaro. I have sent Kempt and Ross to hang upon their rear. The first Léger and our Light Infantry met with bayonets at the charge. The first were almost annihilated.

The lack of cavalry on our side was lamented by David Stewart. He said that the Light Infantry's and the Highlanders' pursuit had been in vain; 'the fugitives ran too swiftly; neither the Highlanders with their light loose garb, nor the Light Infantry, could overtake them. I have more than once had occasion to mention that few things increase a man's speed more effectually than the terror of a bayonet or bullet in his rear . . .' The plain of Maida would have been most favourable for cavalry operations – but as so often in military operations overseas, the insufficiency of transports did not allow all the troops needed to be conveyed. The 20th Light Dragoons arrived the day after the battle.

Leading the Light Infantry which were to harry the retreating French was Colborne who had taken over command of the Light Company of the 20th in succession to McLean. He reminisced later:

We were going on towards a town called Borgia, and were not at all

> certain where the French were. I commanded the advanced guard – about 87 soldiers and two dragoons. I had only one other officer with me. The column was some way behind us, and my guide was getting frightened, so I said, 'Well, I can't help it; if you don't show us the way, or get another guide, you must be hanged.' So he went with two or three soldiers and tried to knock up somebody in a cottage. At last a man was found who said he would lead us if we would let him go when we were within a hundred yards of the town. When we were within sight of the town he took care to put us in mind of our engagement, and we let him go. Then I had not the least idea whether the French were there or not. Just at the entrance to the town I saw a man, so I said, 'There, catch him! make haste!' We ran after him and tried to catch him, but he ran into a cottage, and the same thing happened with two or three others, until we actually found ourselves halfway up the town. At last we found a man who happened to be the Capo Genti, the head of the town, so I said *'Dove sono i Francesi?'* 'Oh, they passed through five or six hours ago, and are encamped a few miles further on.' Then all the people, when they found we were English, came flocking round us, and I had begun to take lodgings for us all, when a message came from our column that it had retreated. Hearing rockets and fireworks they had thought it must be the enemy, when really it was the people in the town firing for joy of our arrival. The retreat of our column was a great pity. The French retired still further the next day, and the people in the town were very angry with us, because, in my expectation of the column, I had ordered 4,000 rations. They all turned and reproached us, and I was anxious as to what would happen. I said, 'It is not my fault. I am very sorry indeed to go back.' But they were very angry all the same. So after marching all day and all night, at four o'clock we had to march back again.

Colborne had reached Borgia, on the Ionian Sea, only ten miles from Catanzaro where Reynier was trying to rally his remnant.

Sir John Stuart had been at Maida composing his dispatch and a proclamation to the army:

> Plains of Maida 6th July 1806
>
> Major General Sir John Stuart finds himself incapable of expressing to the troops the sentiments excited in him by their brave and intrepid conduct in the late action of the fourth, in which they gained so signal a triumph over a boasting and insolent enemy. Their distinguished

behaviour on this memorable day will endear them in the breasts of their grateful countrymen. It will insure them the applause of their approving sovereign and will add another immortal wreath to the laurels of the British army. The Light Battalion under Lt Col Kempt who charged the Enemy's favourite Light Corps, displayed a combined instance of gallantry and discipline of which military records have furnished but few examples.

The 78th and 81st regiments under B. G. Acland shared the first and severest part of the action with the Light Infantry whom they were ordered to support. The gallant and good conduct of the Brigadier General in fulfilling this duty was most nobly seconded by the brave regiments under his orders.

The battalion of grenadiers and the twenty-seventh regiment under Brigadier General Cole made a firm and intrepid resistance against a superior force, and the manner of the 27th regiment in throwing back a wing to receive the enemy cavalry was the strongest token of the discipline of that excellent corps.

The 58th and Watteville's regiment under Colonel Oswald and which were brought up as a second line sustained the advanced column with spirit and intrepidity.

The conduct of Lieut Colonel Ross in throwing the 20th regiment into the wood on the enemy's flank while the latter was attempting to turn our left was a prompt display of gallantry and judgment to which the army was most certainly indebted.

The Artillery was well provided and most effectually served under the command of Major Lamoine. From the various public departments of the army, and especially Lieut Colonel Bunbury's the Quarter Master General, Sir John has to acknowledge the most marked and able assistance not only during the continuance of the action itself but in all the arrangements preparatory to its commencements.

No language that the Major General could adopt would bear any proportion to the feelings with which he recurs to all the circumstances of this great and this signal day!!!

Every soldier whom the General has the honour of addressing will have equal right with himself to make the boast hereafter that he bore a part in the glorious battle of Maida.

Chapter Eight

The Sequel

Sir John Stuart had set out for battle as soon as he saw the French in their position above Maida vale. He was induced to advance without waiting for his cavalry and the 20th regiment to arrive because he thought that all Reynier's troops had not yet concentrated. After the battle, the full scale of the victory became apparent. Reynier had had an army of 7,000 men. It may have been an awareness of greatly outnumbering his enemy which had made Reynier so over-confident that instead of waiting in his easily defensible position, he marched down into the plain 'to drive the English into the sea'. But as had happened so often in army operations overseas, the British force was too small: Brigadier General Brodrick arrived from Sicily with reinforcements of 1,200 British and Neapolitan troops and captured Reggio but the total force was not enough to occupy all the territory recovered. Bunbury, writing long after the event, suggested that Sir Sidney Smith should at once have sailed for Gaeta, announced the victory and landed his marines, and that the army should have arrived in transports in front of Naples. This might have caused King Joseph, who had only 3,000 troops there, to abandon Naples – or to have called for help from Masséna whose 12,000 troops were besieging Gaeta. If this course had been followed and had been successful the results would indeed have been splendid. Both Sir John Fortescue and Professor Oman concur with Bunbury in blaming Sir John Stuart for having failed to exploit his victory, but Bunbury's blame is hard to reconcile with Boothby's account of Bunbury's opinion at the time. This is Boothby's description of the deliberations which took place.

> The enemy, who had advanced to meet us from the south, having immediately after the battle retreated northwards to Catanzaro, instead of attempting to cover the country whence he came, it was plain that he no longer thought of defending Lower Calabria, which province with its garrison he thus abandoned to his victorious adversary. Sir John Stuart was strongly minded to pursue these extraordinary advantages,

and with his small unassisted army (for there was no indication of a national rising) to drive the French still further to the north, and increase his footing in the kingdom of Naples. There was certainly more gallantry than prudence about this idea; for when the interests which depend on this little army are considered, the importance of the Island of Sicily at this moment, and our trifling numbers for territorial occupation, there can be no doubt that those about the General, who prevailed with him to be satisfied with the conquest of the province almost touching this important island, with whose safety he was entrusted, did better service by their counsels than they could at that time have rendered by their swords.

Of this number, I believe, was the Quartermaster-General a young man of great acquirement and high military promise; and certainly not the least influential; of them was our own Commandant of the Royal Engineers [Captain Lefebure], whose vigorous and strong professional opinion certainly had great influence, for the Quartermaster-General in reference to it used these emphatic words, 'It has succeeded.' It was in conformity with the decision produced by these counsels that the headquarters had moved to Monte Leone, and the General was now disposed to content himself with placing the province of Lower Calabria upon such a footing of military occupation as would delay its reoccupation even by a very superior force, and to ensure to us for a considerable time both shores of the Straits of Messina.

The troops having come a long way from their seaside base had little camp equipment. 'We bivouacked in the open fields,' Boothby wrote, 'and shared in all respects the fare of the private soldiers. Our mess of raw meat was delivered to us in the same proportion as theirs; our camp kettle hung gipsy-like over a fire of sticks, and each officer's cloak and blanket spread upon the ground served him for a bed and his valise for a pillow, where he lay with his sword by his side . . .'

The danger was malaria. Calabria was perhaps the deadliest place in Europe for malaria. The site of Sybaris is near Cotrone and it is now supposed that the Sybarites perished from malaria rather than from excessive luxury. A French battalion had lost over sixty men in a fortnight and over two hundred invalids had been left in the hospital in Monte Leone. Colborne contracted fever and blamed the Quartermaster-General's department for having assigned his men a site near a marsh. They suffered sixteen deaths. The doctors did not know how to treat malaria and bled for it.

Colborne was bled and had all his hair shaved. It was nearly a year before the army became free of the fever.

In spite of Bunbury's subsequent strictures there can be no doubt that the decision to concentrate on the safety of Sicily and not seek to exploit the victory by any new expedition to the north was correct. Instead of cruising northwards, Sir Sidney Smith had turned south to bombard Scilla, a seemingly impregnable fortress where Reynier's chief engineer had been left to organise the defence. He treated Sir Sidney Smith's summons to surrender with contempt. Gaeta fell to Masséna on 12 July, its gallant commander having been seriously wounded. On the same date Sir John Stuart marched his army to invest Scilla. The transport carrying the wounded back to Sicily had been driven ashore at Scilla, the British being made prisoners. Their exchange was immediate and some of them were able to take part in the siege which shortly began. The castle, at the end of an isthmus, was cannonaded from the sea on two sides by Sir Sidney Smith's guns and Neapolitan gunboats. 'On the arrival of my Commandant,' wrote Boothby, 'all these futile operations died away. The General and the Admiral equally relied upon the resources of his science and the natural energy of his powerful mind . . . No one was suffered to interfere with his plan of operation.' Boothby went with him to have a good view of the castle from where it could all be studied: 'Whilst he stood with his uplifted telescope carefully examining the nature of the defences, a cannonball very nearly struck him and covered him with sand; but he never even lowered his telescope . . . only showed he was aware of the fact by saying, as he continued to look through his glass, 'What asses, to fire in that way at an individual!'

Boothby was sent across the Straits to superintend the embarkation of stores needed for a battery of four 24-pounders which was going to be sited within 150 yards of the castle. Before the heavy guns could be got up, the Light Artillery would be used to destroy as much as possible of the defences. For this purpose, Boothby was employed in erecting a breastwork for two 12-pounders within half-musket shot of their target, an extremely anxious task. The work was almost completed successfully in darkness but when dawn broke the working party was exposed to very brisk musketry fire.

Scilla surrendered on 23 July. Meanwhile Sir John Stuart had sent the 78th on board ship round to the east coast of the Calabrian peninsula.

Island of Maritimo, S by E, 4 miles. HMS Wizard, 16 guns. (Courtesy of The National Maritime Museum, Greenwich)

Cotrone at once surrendered. This was Reynier's last outlying post and had been left isolated with the French hospital and a garrison of 250 Polish troops. Boothby accompanied the 78th, being attached as Chief Engineer to Colonel McLeod and Captain Hoste (HMS *Amphion*). They intercepted dispatches between King Joseph and Reynier ordering the General to retire to Cassano. *Amphion* continued northwards harassing the retreat of the French from Catanzaro, the frigate 'throwing her shot with admirable precision'. On shore, the British were joyously received by the wretched inhabitants whose misery was often shocking. The nobility were most welcoming but they could not conceal fear that the absence of the French would leave them open to the depredations of the brigands who were known as Massi. Their leaders, called *Capitani*, were savage-looking and Colonel McLeod was treating with them in the hope that they would maintain some sort of order. Calabria was certainly in a miserable state, unadministered and at the mercy of bandits. Lowry Cole had some misgiving in sending Church with an escort of 200 Neapolitan cavalry to reconnoitre Nicastro. Church was able to save the family of the syndic from being murdered and had to maintain patrolling throughout the night. Writing home, he said that this had given him more pleasure than any feats of destruction in the battle.

Boothby was sent on a reconnaissance of port towns in the Gulf of Taranto. They sailed in a fast brig, HMS *Wizard*, but she could not venture into the harbour of Tarentum which was guarded by batteries on an island at its mouth. He entered the harbour in a small boat and narrowly escaped being taken prisoner. On his return to Sicily, he submitted his report to the General – but this was not Sir John Stuart who would be leaving on the same boat which was to carry Boothby's letter to his mother.

Lt. General Henry Fox took over command in Sicily on 29 July. He was a brother of the former Foreign Secretry and was accompanied by his family. His house in Messina soon became an example of domestic bliss. Sir John Moore arrived to be second-in-command. Moore was senior to Stuart and Stuart did not wish to be number three; moreover he was believed to have resented Moore having been given greater praise for his part in the battle of Alexandria than he himself had been accorded. He was of course given a hero's welcome in Messina and was created Count of Maida by the King. However, he did not go to the Court at Palermo but slipped away on a ship to Malta, *en route* for England. His reputation in the army was inferior to that which victory had earned him at home. Bunbury quotes with gusto a friend of his (Major Hammill) writing to Hudson Lowe in Capri about Stuart's departure saying, 'I am confident that he takes with him the detestation of the whole army. As an individual he is abhorred and as an officer despised.' Against this, there is Boothby who writes of 'our gallant litle general'. There is no record of the opinion of the private soldier.

On his arrival in England, Stuart was made a Knight of the Bath, awarded a pension of £1,000 a year for life and presented with the freedom of the City of London and a sword of honour at a banquet in the Guildhall. He received a vote of thanks from both Houses of Parliament, the Lord Chancellor saying: 'Reflecting upon the disasters which have fallen upon peaceful princes and populous territories under the pressure of the vast armies of France, I recollect at the same time that they were not defended by British soldiers, and that when the triumphal monuments of Paris record the victories of Austerlitz and Jena, it shall appear upon the less ostentatious journals of a British Parliament, that upon the plains of Maida her choicest battalions fell beneath the bayonets of half the number of our brave countrymen . . .'

Chapter Nine

New Broom

The army left the mainland for Sicily, embarking at Reggio. Cole's brigade had been at Monte Leone where malaria had again proved deadly; Lieutenant Colonel Johnstone and eight officers of the 58th had died. A small British garrison was left at Scilla, 200 strong under Major George Duncan Robertson. He had commanded the light infantry and battalion companies of the 35th in Kempt's brigade at Maida and with his adjutant Lieutenant John Hatfield, also of the 35th, succeeded in holding Scilla throughout a siege by 6,000 French without losing a single prisoner. Scilla did not capitulate until 17 February 1808.*

Sir Sidney Smith had not been sorry to see Sir John Stuart's departure but he was utterly mistaken if he supposed that he would find support for his policy from Fox and Moore. His flagship, the *Pompée*, had been damaged in an incident which well illustrates his personal bravery. While cruising along the coast, he had seen a French flag on an old watch-tower. He had ordered the ship to be run in to pound the enemy out, and had then gone to his cabin to write letters. The *Pompée*'s broadsides had been returned from the watch-tower and the Captain had interrupted the Admiral to tell him that a Lieutenant and a midshipman had been killed and forty-three men were wounded. Sir Sidney, who had been calmly writing, looked surprised and ordered the marines to land and take the enemy battery from the rear. As soon as the boats touched the shore a number of men had run out waving a white cloth. They said they had been longing to desert but as the British warship had opened fire on them without asking them to surrender they had been compelled to use their gun to the best of their ability.

Bunbury had had a sharp attack of malaria and Sir John Moore invited

* The Seige of Scilla

him to accompany him on a cruise in the frigate *Apollo* as an opportunity to recover his health. Moore, leaving Bunbury in *Apollo*, went to call on Sir Sidney in the crippled *Pompée*. He found that Sir Sidney fancied himself as a man who was directing a formidable campaign. To hear him, one would suppose that nothing but the want of money and arms was preventing him from driving the French from lower Italy and replacing Ferdinand on the throne of Naples. Moore had difficulty in explaining that General Fox did not intend to have his army tied up in defending Calabria. The Calabrese and the Court of Palermo had had a fair opportunity as a consequence of Maida to guard their country. Unfortunately, the Calabrese were divided among themselves, many persons of property favouring the French. The King's supporters included the massi whose *Capitani* were drawn from renegades and banditti of the lowest type. The Commander-in-Chief had therefore decided that the defence of Sicily was his first duty and he must beg Sir Sidney to desist from interfering in the affairs of the Calabrese.

On his return journey south, *Apollo* called at several places on the coast. Moore found the inhabitants terrified and disheartened, running up royalist or republican colours as they thought wisest, and with the arms distributed by Sir Sidney, massacring and pillaging one another. When Moore was back in Sicily, he received a letter from Sir Sidney Smith who 'with his usual impudence' expressed the hope that *Apollo's* cruise along the coast had led Moore 'to think with him'. Fox wrote firmly to the admiral repeating his opinion that British interference in Calabria only gave 'an opportunity to the lawless and vicious to oppress the better sort of inhabitants, encouraging a disposition to revolt that will not in any way assist our cause and will bring a tenfold vengeance on them from the French . . .' He then wrote home about the 'impossibility of acting in concert with' Sir Sidney Smith who at last on 25 January 1807 was instructed by the Admiralty to go to Malta and receive further orders from Collingwood.

The entire Cabinet had considered the circumstances of the admiral's behaviour at the time of Maida. There were three grounds on which they considered that he should be rebuked:

1. His having, without the concurrence of the British Minister in Sicily, accepted a commission from the Government in Palermo.
2. His having taken upon himself the command or direction of an insur-

rection in Calabria destined to co-operate with British troops under the command of a British general.

3. The issuing, and his acting under, the proclamation of the Court of Sicily which had been directly remonstrated against by the British Minister.

Lord Grenville agreed with Windham that any reprimand to Sir Sidney should be as mild as possible. Thanks not only to Windham's personal friendship but to the resilience of Sir Sidney's character, he was shortly able to forward to Collingwood 'a flattering testimonial from the Court of Palermo' and a request to be given permission to accept the Grand Cross of the Order of St Ferdinand, 'as granted to my ever-lamented predecessor in that local service, Lord Nelson'. Smith's next appointment must have been congenial to him because it included the task of transporting the Portuguese royal family to Brazil.

Colborne, having recovered from his illness, was at a turning point in his career. He was made General Fox's Military Secretary – 'a confidential post, and thirty shillings per diem in addition to my pay as Captain – but it is no sinecure.' He had aspired to the post of Military Secretary and had set himself to self-improvement from the time when he was wounded in north Holland in 1799. After being wounded, he was nursed in a house of a priest with whom he had no common language but Latin and had studied French, Italian and Spanish. He had been an ardent admirer of Moore since those days and when Fox left he naturally was to become Moore's Military Secretary. Of course Colborne kept in touch with his brother officers of the 20th and he heard with great amusement of an incident after the arrival of fresh troops from England which included a battalion of the 52nd Light Infantry. The veteran officers of the 20th soon became rather bored by hearing about the model regiment from Shorncliffe.

> The 20th invited the 52nd to dinner. Now there was a young officer of the 52nd by the name of Diggle – very correct, very eager to learn. Two young brutes of the 20th got him between them at dinner, and as the hour for toasts arrived, they explained how curious and interesting were some of the traditions and customs of old regiments. As the junior guest here that night in the mess of the 20th, it would fall to his lot to rise and give the invariable toast 'Confusion to all general officers!' Poor little Diggle did not much like the sound of his duty, but at the right moment, up he got, and addressing Colonel Ross at

the head of his table, said, 'President, I have a toast to propose.' His nerve then failed him, and he got the words wrong. 'Damn all general officers!' piped Diggle. There had been a terrible scandal, and after a meeting of officers the Colonel of the 52nd had almost agreed to turn Diggle out of the regiment. However, Colonel Ross had come forward with an explanation, and since the great alarm of the 52nd was that anything of the story should come to the ears of Sir John Moore, it had been hushed up.

Chapter Ten

Consequences

In Fortescue's opinion, Reynier was not a bad general. He was pompous and conceited and made the mistake of despising his enemy, Charles Rathbone. Low considered that Stuart sometimes 'betrayed an over-hot Scottish temperament' and, if Reynier had kept his high ground, 'would probably have been guilty of an imprudence in order to get at him'. There was personal antagonism between Sir John Stuart and Reynier, the latter having written contemptuously of the British in a book about the campaign in Egypt: Reynier had cast the blame for his defeat on Abdallah Menon under whom he had been serving. Paul-Louis Courier had been sent to Taranto so was not at Maida. When he heard that Reynier had been defeated *('bien rossé')* he ascribed it in part to Reynier having been controlled by the presence of Lebrun, of the '*troupe d'orée*', as an ADC. If Reynier had not gone to attack, the fashionable ADC would have raised the cry against him in Paris. 'A silly thing (*sotte chose*) indeed for a general who commands to have on his shoulders an ADC of the Emperor, a fine gentleman of the Court, and bringing you in his pocket the genius of his imperial Majesty! Reynier had a surveillant put over him, to give an account of what should happen . . . Had the battle been gained, then it would have been the Emperor's doing . . . But if the battle is lost, why, then it is our fault! The golden troop of courtiers will say "The Emperor was not there!"'

Reynier's explanation for having lost the battle of Maida was that his troops had flinched – which had been patently untrue. King Joseph Bonaparte's explanation published in Naples was simple – a big lie. He announced that the British had had an army 9,000 strong supplemented by 3–4,000 Calabrese brigands: '*Les Anglais étaient treize mille et nous avions cinq mille cinquant*!' Added to the British force was Ross's disembarkment of 2,500! Reynier had witnessed the success of line over column in the battles before Alexandria and should have known better. He would use his familiar tactics again in the Peninsula, leading Napoleon to write after Busaco: 'Ney and Masséna had never seen the English before: but that Reynier, whom they have already thrashed twice, should have attacked in this way is simply astounding.' Years later in St Helena Napoleon expanded on this theme, recalling how at the beginning of the war the French had held English soldiers in contempt. He supposed Reynier had thought that the British would run away and be driven into the sea, adding that Reynier 'was a man of talent, but more fit to give command to an army of twenty-five or thirty thousand men, than to command one of five or six'. Napoleon himself never saw British soldiers in action until Waterloo.

By contrast, the British learnt lessons from the battle which were successfully applied throughout the Peninsular War. Cole, Kempt, Oswald, Ross and Colborne all distinguished themselves; it was Colborne who made the final attack on the French guard at Waterloo. The greatest gain of all was in morale. As Colborne put it in a letter home, 'The loss of the French in killed, wounded and prisoners, is almost incredible, nearly 2,000. Our army entered the field with 4,600, the enemy had 7,200 bayonets and 300 cavalry. Fortunate it is for us that the spectators were numerous. I now begin to think, as our ancestors did, that one Englishman is equal to two Frenchmen.' An article in the 1929 issue of the regimental magazine of the Lancashire Fusiliers said of the battle, 'It broke the spell of invincibility that so long had attached to Napoleon's armies . . . For years, all ranks celebrated the anniversary of the action, and used decorations of myrtle, being allowed to wear sprigs in their caps, in remembrance of the Plain of Maida which was covered with myrtle bushes.'

If Craig had still been in command, it seems unlikely that an expeditionary force would have set out from Sicily. Craig's nature was more cautious than Stuart's. Stuart's main strategic objective was to ensure the security of Sicily by winning a battle and destroying the batteries and magazines assembled for invasion: a possible by-product might be the relief of pressure on Gaeta; if Reynier were defeated, Masséna might be forced to raise the siege. This would accord well with the schemes of Sir Sidney Smith who despite Collingwood's orders to him clung to the conviction, based on his uncontradictable because unwitnessed death-bed conversation with Pitt, to the effect that the secret high purpose of British policy was to restore the Bourbon monarchy at Naples. Smith's behaviour after Maida in turning south insted of cruising north appears to give the lie to the sincerity of his conviction. Whatever his dreams may have been, they were doomed to unfulfilment by his failure to collaborate with Stuart in detailed planning

The Maida Medal (courtesy of the Director, National Army Museum)

and his absence from the scene when the invading army sailed. The concurrence of Fortescue and Oman in Bunbury's lament that Sir John Stuart failed to follow up his victory seems to ignore the limited resources available to the commanders for amphibious operations. There had not been enough sea-transports to convey all the troops intended for the expeditionary force, so there was no cavalry. There certainly were not sufficient troops or ships for neutralizing Lower Calabria and sustaining a seaborne assault on Naples.

Fortescue in his history describes Stuart as 'not without brains and by no means without ability' but 'vain, flighty and superficial'. Yet in his introduction to the 1927 edition of Bunbury's *Narratives of some passages in the Great War with France*, Fortescue was most disparaging. He appears to have been wrong in supposing that the Court of Palermo worked upon the feelings of Sir John Stuart. Stuart did not visit Palermo from Messina and there is no record of his having met the Queen before Maida except at the Castellammare review in November 1805. In his dignified protest to Smith after having been informed by the latter of his Royal Commission as Viceroy of the Calabrias, Stuart wrote that as 'commander of a British army' he 'would act perfectly independently of the Court of Palermo and its Councils'. On his later return to the Mediterranean as commander-in-chief he would naturally have dealings with the Court and he had no illusions about its rottenness. Bunbury records his making a tirade against it at a dinner party in Ischia in 1809 – 'As for the King, his cause is desperate; he has lost one kingdom, and he must lose the other. There is no alternative for England but to take Sicily herself, or to abandon it altogether.' Bunbury was not surprised by the sentiments, which he had often heard before, but by Stuart expressing them in company. Fortescue is unjust in bracketing Stuart with Smith and intemperate in describing both as 'brother impostors of the two services' and 'posturing commanders'.

One must conclude that Stuart had done well to seize his short 'opportunity for glory'. He had known that General Fox was on his way to Sicily; Fox actually arrived a fortnight after the battle. Oman wrote that he knew of no other war 'in which, after a decisive victory, the victors and the vanquished turned their backs on each other, and proceeded to place 150 miles between them'. A parallel perhaps took place some eighteen hundred years earlier in Agricola's campaign at the northernmost edge of the Roman

Empire when after defeating the Picts at Mons Graupias the Romans returned to a defendable line further south.

A gold medal was struck for Maida by order of King George III. This was an innovation, the first campaign medal.* It was awarded only to seventeen officers. When at last in 1848 the Army General Service medal was approved for all ranks who had been in campaigns between 1793 and 1814, a clasp for 'Maida' was given to all survivors.

Finally, the longest-lasting consequence of the victory: the name Maida was given in 1807 to a stretch of the Edgware Road near the new Regent's Canal, later the whole length of road between the canal and Kilburn becoming Maida Vale.

* The Maida Medal

Appendices

Appendix A: Sources

Henry **Bunbury** (1778 – 1860). He was chief staff officer to Sir John Stuart. He had been ADC to the Duke of York and had come out to the Mediterranean as Craig's Assistant Quartermaster-General.

Roveara. He was brigade-major to Lowry Cole who was Sir John Stuart's second-in-command and commanding the 1st Brigade composed of the Grenadier Battalion and the 27th Regiment. Roveara was a Swiss patriot who had probably been serving in De Watteville's Regiment in Malta when Cole appointed him. He was to remain with Cole, to whom he was devoted, until he was killed at Sauroren in 1813.

John Colborne. At the time of Maida he was twenty-seven and was serving in the Light Battalion under Kempt on the right of the British army. He belonged to a Hampshire family and had been left an orphan when thirteen. There had been an idea of his taking Holy Orders but he was delighted on leaving Winchester to hear that his step-father had obtained an ensigncy for him in the 20th Regiment. At that date the 20th was the East Devonshire Regiment and three-quarters of its members were drawn from seven counties. Colborne had his baptism of fire in the North Holland campaign of 1799 and did extremely well. He was to rise to the rank of Field Marshal and be made Lord Seaton, winning every step of promotion without purchase. He was a good letter writer.

Richard Church (1784 – 1873). He had been commissioned at the age of thirteen and had come to favourable notice in the Egyptian campaign of 1801. In Malta he had been made adjutant of the Light Infantry Battalion commanded by Kempt and Sir John Stuart later appointed him to be

Kempt's brigade-major. He was a good linguist and a natural choice for being selected to carry out a reconnaissance in Calabria after the battle. In his later career he was a leading figure in the liberation of Greece.

E. Charlton. He served in the 61st Regiment and wrote a journal of the Regiment's activities between 1804 and 1851. He was not with the Light Company (the only company of the regiment which fought at Maida) but remained in Sicily until after the battle. His unpublished journal which includes several anecdotes about the campaign is in the Regiments of Gloucestershire Museum.

Charles Steevens. The 20th Regiment, all excepting its Light Company, did not sail with the main expeditionary force to the Gulf of St Eufemia but were embarked in feluccas, large open boats, as part of a deception plan to mislead the French into thinking that the invasion was to be made at the southernmost end of Calabria, between Reggio and Cape Spartivento. Steevens was with the main body of the regiment and arrived in the bay to land at the nearest place to where the battle was actually taking place. The 20th's timely intervention was decisive.

Charles Boothby, the Sapper officer quoted as witnessing Sir John Stuart's own embarkation, was left with a small defending force at the Bastione di Malta to guard against possible counter-attack and was engaged in strengthening it with sandbags and a surrounding ditch on both sides as far as the shore. He was not near enough to see the battle but as soon as word came to him of victory he was able to rush to the battlefield.

Three other main sources were not contemporaries but military historians writing afterwards:

(i) **Sir John Fortescue**, the magisterial historian of the British army.

(ii) **Charles Rathbone Low** who wrote *The Great Battles of the British Army*. His chapter about Maida is specially valuable because he visited the battlefield ten years after the event when it still held many relics and he spoke to numerous eye-witnesses of the clash between the two armies.

(iii) **Professor C. W. C. Oman** (later **Sir Charles Oman**) who on 28 November 1907 gave a lecture in the Royal Artillery Institution called 'An historical sketch of the battle of Maida'. Oman had examined the French archives including the unpublished dispatch of General Ebenezer Reynier (1771 – 1814). By his analysis of the French 'morning states' he was able to establish the exact numbers of French troops present at Maida and of the casualties.

Appendix B: British Order of Battle

The composition of the expeditionary force which set out from Sicily was:

Commander: Major General Sir John Stuart

Deputy Quartermaster-General: Lieutenant Colonel Henry Bunbury

Military Secretary: Captain de Sade

Chief Engineer: Captain Lefebure

Unattached: 20 men of 20th Light Dragoons

1st Brigade: Brigadier General Lowry Cole

Grenadier Battalion (Grenadier companies of 20th, 27th, 35th, 58th, 81st and De Watteville's)

2nd Brigade: Brigadier General Acland

2/78th and 81st (less its Grenadier and Light companies)

3rd Brigade (Reserve): Lieutenant Colonel Oswald

58th (8 companies), De Watteville's (8 companies)

Light Brigade: Lieutenant Colonel Kempt

Light companies and flanker companies of 20th, 27th, 35th, 58th, 61st, 81st and De Watteville's; 150 men from 3 battalion companies of 35th; 2 companies of Corsican Rangers; 1 company of Royal Sicilian Volunteers

8 companies of the 20th Foot under Lieutenant Colonel Ross had an independent role.

Royal Artillery: Major Lemoine

10 4-pounders

4 6-pounders

2 howitzers

Each regiment had on its establishment 1 surgeon with 2 assistants. The total strength of the British force was approximately 5,790 all ranks.

The names of the infantry regiments under the 1881 reforms which carried the battle honour 'Maida' were:

Lancashire Fusiliers

Royal Inniskilling Fusiliers

Royal Sussex Regiment

Northamptonshire Regiment

Gloucestershire Regiment

Seaforth Highlanders

Loyal Regiment (North Lancashire)

All have since been merged to make bigger units.

Appendix C: French Order of Battle

The French army under General Ebenezer Reynier was organized in three brigades:

Brigade Compère:

1st Léger

42nd Ligne

Brigade Digonet:

23rd Léger

1st Polonais

Brigade Peyri:

1st Swiss

9th Chausseurs à cheval

One horse battery

Total strength approximately 7,200

Notes

1. (page 21) **Lineage of Sir John Stuart (1759 – 1815) Count of Maida**

The *Dictionary of National Biography* names Sir John Stuart's father as Colonel John Stuart (1700–79) who went to America with General Oglethorpe in 1753 and became Superintendent of Indian Affairs in the Southern Department of North America. He married Sarah Fenwick of Charleston, South Carolina. Having fought on the Loyalist side in the war of independence, his property was confiscated and he returned to England. His son John was sent to school at Westminster and was commissioned in the 3rd Foot Guards in 1778.

Alone in the galaxy of roughly contemporary generals called Stewart, the *DNB* makes no mention of his lineage. He was in fact a grandson of John Steuart (1676–1759), Bailie of Inverness. This family was descended from King Robert II through Alexander Stewart, the Wolf of Badenoch, and held the barony of Kinchardine in Strathspey until 1661. The Bailie always spelt his name Steuart. His son appears to have dropped the e after leaving Scotland and this is a good illustration of the sameness of the name in its different spellings. The Letter-Book of Bailie John Steuart has as its frontispiece a reproduction of two miniatures showing Count Maida and his sister.

2. (page 29) **The British army at Maida**

The order of battle is shown at Appendix B. It included three foreign units:

De Watteville's Swiss

This regiment was formed in 1801 under Baron Frederic de Watteville from the remnants of the Swiss force which had tried to oppose the French attack on Berne. Its colonel was Baron Louis de Watteville and the officers were mostly Bernese aristocrats. Its first existing pay-list is dated May 1801 and the regiment reached Malta in July 1801. All ranks maintained a high standard of discipline and efficiency and were a credit to the British army.

The regiment served in Canada before its disbandment and was granted the use of 'Maida' as a battle honour.

Royal Corsican Rangers
The Corsican Rangers were raised at Minorca in 1799 and served in Moore's Reserve Brigade in Egypt. They were disbanded in 1802. The Brigade's former commanding officer, Hudson Lowe, raised the Royal Corsican Rangers, consisting of ten companies, in 1803. They were disbanded in 1817. By this date their colonel, Hudson Lowe, had been posted to be Napoleon's keeper as Governor of St Helena, an appointment which some wit described as appropriate because he was accustomed to dealing with unruly Corsicans.

Royal Sicilian Volunteers
The one company which fought with the 'flankers' in Kempt's brigade seems to have been a unit of the Sicilian army integrated for the expedition with the British army. Sir John Stuart had with him a Sicilian marchese as an extra ADC. The Sicilians would have made good soldiers if trained and led by British officers and NCOs but the Queen would not countenance any recruitment until the mid-summer of 1806 when Sir John Stuart obtained permission to raise a corps of 500 Sicilian Fencibles drawing British pay and wearing British uniform. By order of the Horse Guards 23 July 1806 it was directed that a company of Sicilians 100 strong should be raised and attached to each of the regiments serving in or going to the Mediterranean. Major George Duncan Robertson, commanding the garrison at Scilla, and the British soldiers with him, were transferred to the Sicilian Regiment in which Robertson was promoted Lieutenant Colonel. Robertson was later to succeed his father as Chief of Clan Donnachaid.

David Stewart was critical of using foreign troops 'in situations where their failure must endanger the safety or success of an army . . . It is not easy to see the necessity of placing foreign troops, many of whom have deserted their own standards, among the choice of the British army, before their courage and fidelity had been fairly proved. I believe General Stuart heartily repented the arrangement he had made.'

3. (page 40) The French Swiss Regiment being mistaken for the British

According to Paul-Louis Courier, some of whose letters are quoted by Bunbury, the French de Watteville's Regiment was again mistaken for British shortly after the battle. They were leading the retreat of the battered French army when they reached Cassano. The inhabitants came out to greet them and congratulated them 'on having trounced the rascally French'. They were not recognized until they fired on the townsmen at point-blank range. Fifty-two of the inhabitants were taken to be shot that evening in the square of Cassano, the executions being performed by compatriots who requested the task as a favour in the interests of their internecine feuding. 'Such are the feasts of Syparis,' commented Courier.

4. (page 41) Memorandum left by Stewart of Garth 1828

These two documents appear to be a memorial written for submission through the proper channels to the King of the Two Sicilies. The earlier one was written by the general; the authorship of the one dated 14 July 1828 is unknown, but its probable author was Macdonell of Glengarry.

Private memorandum

Major General Stewart had an opportunity of performing some important pieces of service at the battle of Maida. The circumstances being of such a nature that a public notice of them might be injurious to the character of some brother officers, long dead, he has foreborne speaking of the subject and cautioned the Officers who were present to do the same; and now he will only state a few brief particulars.

After the enemy had been driven by the first charge at the battle of Maida, Major Stewart observed that the Officer commanding the 81st Regiment did not seem to understand or to act to his instructions; he therefore rode to his part of the field and remonstrating with him, a remedy was instantly applied, and by this timely interference, was prevented a serious calamity which might have affected the character of that officer, and the general success of the day.

When Major Stewart returned from this duty to his own regiment, he found that the place it had occupied in the field was vacant, and that a close column of Companies was forming on the right. Riding up to this intended column, he saw four companies in columns and the others were following up to complete this formation.

Surprised at this unexpected movement, he asked the cause, when the Commanding Officer informed him that he had received orders to retreat from the field. Seeing that he was determined to obey the orders as he conceived it to be, and was proposing to march to the rear, Major Stewart hurried away to the General Commanding the Brigade, and begged him to recall the order, adding that the enemy had already been forced to fly by three separate charges with the bayonet, and had retreated upwards of two miles – that if these advantages were followed up, the victory would be complete, and the enemy driven from the field; which was already so strewed with their dead and wounded that it required attention to keep clear of the bodies when riding through them, but that if the order was persevered in, the enemy would resume their confidence, return to the charge, and occupy the ground vacated by the Highlanders and thus cut off the communications between the Light Infantry and the 81st Regiment, attack them in detail and obtain that victory which the British had all but gained. The Brigade General answered that he had given no such order, and that there must have been some mistake. Major Stewart hastily rode back to his regiment, and found all but one company formed in close column ready to march off. He ordered the columns to face to the right about, to front the enemy, and to form line, and to open a fire the instant each company got into line. During this time the enemy acted as was anticipated, and had advanced with an intention of occupying the vacant space. This movement brought them so much within reach of musketry, and so correct and deadly was the aim of our young soldiers, that in ten minutes the field in their front was cleared of the Enemy, and with a number of killed almost unprecedented in proportion to the number engaged. Thus the misapprehension or mistake about orders turned out to be highly advantageous; and Major Stewart learned afterwards from a French Officer, that it was considered by them as an able manoeuvre or ruse from which they suffered most severely.

Fearful, as he has already observed, that the circumstances if known would prove injurious to the Officers, Major Stewart requested of General Sir John Stuart not to represent the case to the Secretary of State as he expressed a wish to do, in justice, as he said, to an Officer to whom he owed so much – for the question rested upon this, whether Maida was to be an honourable achievement, or a thorough defeat, – but that disaster was prevented.

Now as twenty two years has elapsed and as the present representation is intended for a foreign power which will not ask for names; Major General Stewart trusts that there is no impropriety in mentioning the subject thus confidentially.

London 12th July 1828

Second memorandum

The circumstances under which the battle of Maida was fought and its important results as connected with the Kingdom of Naples are well known. The striking inferiority of numbers on the part of the British gave additional brilliancy to their success over an Army composed of veteran and hitherto invincible troops, commanded by an Officer of such acknowledged talents and experience as General Regnier – The disparity of numbers was considerable; the British force being 4750 men and 60 artillerymen with three small field pieces; that of the French 7500, with 300 cavalry and a train of artillery. – The field of battle was an open plain with an even surface, offering no obstruction to the advance of either side. – Both were drawn up (each in two lines) in the centre of the plain. The first line of the enemy from their superior numbers extended considerably beyond both flanks of the British front line, which consisted of three corps – the Light Infantry Battalion on the right, the 78th Highland regiment in the centre, and the 81st Regiment on the left; the whole amounting to 2150 men. – The French first line of 3900 men was drawn up in a similar and parallel order directly to the front of the British and, at the distance of about 600 yards. – Leaving the second line, consisting of the Grenadier battalion and the 27th Regiment, considerably in the rear, the first line commenced the attack by a forward movement in slow time till within 300 yards of the enemy, when they rushed forward in double quick time, charged with the bayonet, and drove the French back to within a short distance of their second line. After a short pause, to allow the soldiers to recover breath and to reform the line correctly, they charged again, and with such effect that the first line of the enemy was driven back on the second, and both being intermingled retreated in great confusion, but endeavouring to rally and offer an opposing front, they were again charged and driven back with great loss. At this period the British second line marched up and formed on the left of the first line, when the whole advanced; and charging the enemy with increased vigour, compelled them to retreat in such irretrievable disorder, that, despairing of being able to make any further resistance, they threw away their arms, and fled with a speed which could not be overtaken, sustaining, however, a loss of 930 men killed, and 1146 so severely wounded, that they could not leave the field, besides a number of slightly wounded who escaped to their rear, while the loss of the British was only 1 officer and 41 soldiers killed, and 11 officers and 269 soldiers wounded, being in the proportion of 30 killed of the French to 1 of the British. The Battalion of the 78th Highland Regiment, stationed in the centre of the first line, had only been a short time recruited and formed, and when they thus successfully opposed the veteran troops of France little more than a twelvemonth after they had left their native mountains. Upwards of 600 of them were under twenty years of age, and with so little experience that they had hardly sufficient knowledge of the English language to comprehend the drill instructions. Lieutenant Colonel Macleod [killed the following year in Egypt] commanded the 78th Regiment early in the action, but being wounded, Major David Stewart, now Major General and Governor and Commander in Chief of St Lucia, commanded, but he being also severely wounded, the command fell upon Major James Macdonell, now a Colonel in the Army and Lieutenant Colonel of His Majesty's Coldstream Regiment of Guards, who completed the duty, and pursued the enemy in their flight. These facts along with others are humbly submitted to the consideration of the King of Naples in the hope that the consequence of the importance of the battle fought and gained in his Dominions, and in support of his Crown and dignity His Majesty will be graciously pleased to grant some mark of distinction to the two surviving field officers, Major General David Stewart and Colonel James Macdonell; – not on account of any merit they presume to claim for themselves, but as a testimony of approval of the unyielding firmness displayed by the brave youths* they had the honor and good fortune to command on that occasion, – the first check that was given in the last war to the supposed invincibility of the French troops, and the forerunner of the many great and glorious actions which have so eminently contributed to give stability to the name and character of the British Arms.

The King of Great Britain has been graciously pleased to give medals,

* Later fate of a Seaforth drummer-boy

and the order of the Companion of the Bath to Major General Stewart and Colonel Macdonell, – One of the medals was on account of the battle of Maida, the first action for which medals have been granted by His Majesty to the officers of his Army.

London 14th July, 1828

5. (page 57) **The siege of Scilla**

Major Robertson and his small garrison defended Scilla with great skill. He had steps cut in the living rock which provided a staircase from the waterside to the gate of the castle hidden from the view of the enemy. Eventually the stronghold was lost by treachery, Neapolitan gunboats having deserted to the French. The British commander-in-chief by this date was Sherbrooke who had watched incredulously as the gunboats crossed over the Straits of Messina. He arraigned the Colonel-Commandant of the Neapolitan arsenal who had allowed them to leave: 'I don't know what your government will do with you. You are not under my command, luckily for you; for if you were, by God, I would try you by a drum-head court-martial and hang you up within half an hour.'

6. (page 65) **The Maida Medal**

The Maida Medal was struck in 1808 by order of King George III. It was awarded to seventeen officers. It was in gold and circular, of much artistic merit. The obverse showed an effigy of the King above the legend 'Georgius Tertius Rex'. The reverse bore an animated figure of Britannia standing between the word Maida and the Manx-like arms – which are legs – of Sicily. The medal, which was issued with glass faces, had a ribbon which was claret with blue edges; it was intended to be suspended from the button-hole.

It was not until 1848 that the Army General Service Medal was struck as an award for men who had fought in the wars between 1793 and 1814. A clasp with the word 'Maida' was issued to all survivors of the battle. The ribbon was deep crimson edged with blue.

7. (page 77) **Later fate of a Seaforth drummer-boy**

The 78th were part of the army which went to Egypt in 1807 under Major General Mackenzie Fraser. The British Consul in Alexandria, Major Ernest Missett, gave completely misleading information to the general, as a consequence of which a detachment including five companies of the 78th under

Lieutenant Colonel Macleod were sent to El Hamet where they were trapped and mostly killed. Some were taken prisoner. David Stewart wrote:

> . . . An extraordinary scene followed in the struggle and assembling of the enemy for prisoners, who, according to the custom of the Turks, became the private property of the person who took them, and for each of whom a ransom was expected.

When Kinglake, author of *Eothen*, reached Cairo he stayed at the house of Effendi Osman, an ex-dragoman in the British Consulate. Osman had in fact been a drummer-boy at Maida, John McLeod. He had been spared his life at El Hamet on condition of converting to Islam. He had afterwards done well in the Arabian religious war against the Wahabis, who a century later were to triumph under Ibn Saud who gave his name to the country. His freedom came about after a chance meeting in Jedda with J.-L. Burckhardt, the Swiss explorer who was the first western traveller in modern times to see Petra. Burckhardt was on his way in disguise to Mecca. He was able to buy Osman and took him with him to Cairo where employment as a dragoman in the British Consulate was obtained.

At the date of Kinglake's visit to Cairo Osman had prospered

> having acquired property and become *effendi*, or gentleman . . . he seemed to be much respected by his brother Mahometans, and gave pledge of his sincere alienation from Christianity by keeping a couple of wives. He affected the same sort of reserve in mentioning them as is generally shown by Orientals. He invited me, indeed, to see his hareem, but he made both his wives bundle out before I was admitted; he felt, as it seemed to me, that neither of them would bear criticism, and I think that this idea, rather than any motive of sincere jealousy, induced him to keep them out of sight. The rooms of the hareem reminded me of an English nursery, rather than of a Mahometan paradise. One is apt to judge of a woman before one sees her, by the air of elegance, or coarseness, with which she surrounds her home; I judged Osman's wives by this test, and condemned them both. But the strangest feature in Osman's character was his inextinguishable nationality. In vain he had suffered captivity, conversion, circumcision – in vain they had passed him through fire in their Arabian campaigns – they could not cut away or burn out poor Osman's inborn love of all that was Scotch; in vain men called him *Effendi* – in vain he swept along in eastern robes – in vain the rival wives adorned his hareem;

> the joy of his heart still plainly lay in this, that he had three shelves of books, and that the books were thoroughbred Scotch – the Edinburgh this – the Edinburgh that, and above all, I recollect he prided himself upon the 'Edinburgh Cabinet Library'.

At the time of Burckhardt's purchase of Osman's freedom, J. S. Buckingham of the British Consulate in Jedda recorded that Osman always carried a small pocket bible inscribed on the flyleaf:

> J. M. – it is my name
> And Scotland is my nation
> Perth it is my native place
> And Christ is my salvation.

Burckhardt died in 1817 leaving his property in Cairo to Osman. Osman died of plague in 1849 and was buried in a Muslim cemetery under the same stone as Burckhardt. Probably neither had been a Muslim at heart.

Bibliography

Acton, Harold. *The Bourbons of Naples* (1965)

Bunbury, Sir Henry. *Narratives of some passages in the Great War with France 1799–1810*

Boothby, Charles. *Under England's Flag from 1804 to 1810* (Adam and Charles Black, London 1900)

Cannon. *Historical Record of the 20th East Devonshire Regiment of Foot*

Charlton, Lt. Col. E., *61st Regiment 1804–51*. Unpublished journal in Regiments of Gloucestershire Museum

Church, E. M. *Chapters in an adventurous life. Sir Richard Church in Italy and Greece* (Blackwood 1895)

Cole, Sir Lowry. *Memoirs* edited by Maud Lowry Cole and Stephen Gwynne (Macmillan 1934)

Coleridge, Samuel Taylor. *Collected Letters*

Courier, Paul-Louis. *Letters*

de Gaury, Gerald. *Travelling Gent. The life of Alexander Kinglake (1809–1891)*

Douglas, Norman. *Old Calabria*

Finley, Milton C. *Prelude to Spain; The Calabrian Insurrection*

Fortescue, Sir John. *A History of the British Army* vol 5 ch XI

Grant, James. *Adventures of an Aide-de-camp* (a romantic novel in which the hero is an imaginary ADC of Sir John Stuart) (1848)

Kinglake, A. W. *Eothen* (1844)

Low, Charles Rathbone. *The Great Battles of the British Army* (1885)

Mackesy, Piers. *The War in the Mediterranean 1803–1810* (1957)

Maclean, Loraine. *Indomitable Colonel* (Shepheard-Walwyn 1986)

Moore Smith, G. C. *The life of John Colborne, Field Marshal Lord Seaton* (John Murray 1903)

Oman, Carola. *Nelson*

Oman, Carola. *Sir John Moore*

Ramage. *The nooks and by-ways of Italy*. (Ramage in South Italy edited by Edith Clay 1965)

Russell of Liverpool, Lord. *Knight of the Sword, the life and letters of Admiral Sir Sidney Smith* (Gollancz 1964)

Steevens, Charles. *Reminiscences of my military life from 1795 to 1818 by the late Lt. Col. Charles Steevens formerly of XX Regiment*

Steuart, Bailie John, *The letter-book of Bailie John Steuart*. Scottish History Society, Edinburgh 1915

Stewart, Colonel David. *Sketches of the character, manners and present state of the Highlanders of Scotland* (Edinburgh 1822)

Triman, R. *Historical memoir of the 35th Royal Sussex Regiment of Foot*

Tullibardine, Marchioness of. *A military history of Perthshire 1660–1902*

Articles in Journals

Stevenson, Percy R.: 'Sir Walter Scott and his dogs', *Cornhill Magazine*. December 1919

Oman, C. W. C.: 'An historical sketch of the battle of Maida', *Journal of the Royal Artillery 1908*

Journal of the Society for Army Historical Research, vol. XXI no. 84 to vol. XXII no. 92: articles on foreign units

Haythornthwaite, Philip J.: 'Swiss Corps in British Service 1794–1816', *Military Historical Services Bulletin* vol. 24 no. 94 Nov 1973

'The Battle of Maida', *The Gallipoli Gazette* (Lancashire Fusiliers magazine) July 1929

The Stewarts vol III: article on Major General David Stewart CB of Garth and Drumcharry

Historical record of the 81st Regiment or Loyal Lincoln Volunteers (Gibraltar 1872)

Short History of the 58th Regiment

Atlantic Ocean
London
Amsterdam
Ostend
Antwerp
Dunkirk
Brussels
Aix-la-Chapelle
Rhine
Paris
Angers
Nantes
FRANCE
SPAIN
Ebro
Madrid
Lisbon
Carthagena
Rhône
Milan
Piacenza
Savona
Genoa
Marseilles
Nice
Toulon
Corsica
Majorca
Sardinia
Sicily